Life of Compounding Interest

Investing Toward a Good Life as an Average Person

Reid Pierpoint

Cover by Sarah Duke

Copyright © 2025

All rights reserved.

ISBN:979-8-9994427-1-0

DEDICATION

This book was written for the young people in my life: My daughters and my siblings.

The best advice you receive will be sought, not volunteered. You will receive an enormous amount of guidance throughout your life, some good and some bad; most of it will be well-intentioned. However, these things will teach you what you ought to know. There will be times in life where you realize that there are things that there are things you want and need to know, leading you to seek your own answers. Having someone to ask challenging questions to is a luxury I hope you acquire. Should that person be me, know that I have been there, looked up, and found myself without guidance.

When you look up and I am not there, I want you to have access to some of the wisdom I have gathered on my journey to help you in yours. While I am not successful in material wealth, I have been enormously successful in finding strength, love, and purpose.

This book is written with love and the wish that anyone who reads it can understand the secret to my successes and apply them to live a better life. The idea that the youth have a chance at a better life than their parents materially may seem a fading dream; I wish even happier lives for you, free of the trappings of modern life, extracting only the best parts.

I hope that I can encourage you to act in your own best interest and choose the path of meaning over material, and maybe avoid a few mistakes along the way, no matter how attractive they may seem. I hope that you find your own unique way to make your corner of the world just a bit bigger and brighter, serving as an example to those around you. I hope that my words inspire you to be the light that you wish to see in the world.

CONTENTS

Life Is Simply Growing A Portfolio 1

The Concept Of Capital Essence 13

You Are Your Own Business 23

Take Your Assessments 43

Set Your Goals 73

Stakeholders and Shareholders 97

Know the Costs 119

Avoid Losses, Especially Big Ones 133

Educate Yourself in What Matters 159

Plan for Uncertainty and Capitalize On It 179

Try To Keep Things Simple 195

Foreword:
The Why Is More Important Than The How

So often we do things with all the best intentions, and they still go wrong. Sometimes we try our best, and it isn't quite enough. Sometimes we learn, but it is a bit too late. This is why I chose to write this book.

Growing up, the odds for success were stacked against me to achieve even an average quality of life. I was born to a teenage mother, who managed to raise five children through four different marriages. I saw firsthand struggles and hardship. I received very little education after the second grade and lived in underfunded and impoverished communities. I was brought along for the ride for more bad financial decisions than most, and was very aware of the lack of security that surrounded me throughout my childhood. No matter the situation, though, I was fortunate enough to know there were people in my life in whom I could find love. Maybe not sound advice, but love.

Despite the rough start, I had one goal: to have a family and offer them the life I never had. No wondering where money for food or bills would come from, no questionably safe environments, no wanting education and not being able to obtain it, and no fear of the family breaking up. I moved out as soon as I could and was able to secure a college degree, a decent career, a healthy marriage, and two children of my own. I worked hard to make my dreams come true and shed the behaviors and mindsets that I saw plague my family. I leaned fully into an economic model of thinking, running my life like a small business, always seeking to operate in the black and grow intuitively. Everything could be thought of like money, and there was a logical way to behave and a clear right decision to make.

As a teen and early adult, I spent a lot of time figuring things out on my own. I didn't look much to the adults in my life for advice. However, as a young father, I came to learn that not all decisions can be made with logic. There were things that I did not have a clear reference for. Juggling life and a career, being faced with true moral quandaries, and mounting existential angst, not coming apart at the seams was not easy. I did not have a great father to model after or against, or many other male role models for that matter. Most of the men from my childhood that I held in any regard passed away in my teens. The only man left was my grandfather.

My grandfather was a good man of legendary proportions. He was quiet, mild-tempered, extremely intelligent, marginally successful, lifelong family man, and had the strongest moral character of anyone I had ever known. His father left when he was young and was not a great one. One fact that anyone could tell you about him, but I never heard him spout once, is that he never once drank or did drugs. He built software for some of the largest companies in the state and led teams of engineers throughout the seventies and eighties until he settled down at a bank and was forced into retirement at sixty-five. If anyone had the answers to my questions about life and how to manage through the tough times it was him.

The problem was that he was in the later stages of Alzheimer's disease. He was rarely lucid and was no longer able to give the sound advice that I sought. I had officially waited too long to ask how he handled these things when he was my age, or what to look out for next. Worse, I was reminded of this every time I saw him. I missed my chance to get to know him a little better and allow him to pass on his wisdom.

I have quite a few siblings. They would undoubtedly have some of the same problems and questions I did in a few years, and they, like me, had few if any men in their lives to turn to for advice. I have daughters, and parenting is messy in the trenches. While I do what I can to impart knowledge and wisdom to them, the best I can, freezing thoughts and opinions in time gives me the chance to show them a version of me before I become the man I will be in ten or twenty years' time.

So is this infallible life advice? No. Is it a step-by-step guide to success in life or finances? No. This is simply one man's way of imparting acquired wisdom to the young people in his life. Not facts, but observations and ideas to stimulate thinking. These are simply reflections on the concepts that have served me well in life to this point and continue to guide my decision-making practices. These reflections are fueled by a life of learning from the mistakes of others and my own; mistakes that I would rather not see repeated.

Most importantly, I hope that this can bring some hope to someone who is struggling with life as an average person. There is no shortage of people willing to give advice on how to get rich or become successful at anything fast. While some of it may be true for some, it certainly will not be for most. The truth is that most of the population is average people with average capabilities, bogged down by the complexities and hardships of modern life. Most of us will not become rich. Many more of us will manufacture a level of misery that is just tolerable enough not to change and just barely good enough not to try and escape. There are antidotes for this misery and lack of fulfillment. It isn't fast and it isn't easy, but it is very much worthwhile. Much of it is simply learning to be content.

So I do hope you read on. I hope that you are able to glean some insight that helps guide you through hard times or avoid them altogether. I hope that you find something to disagree with on a logical, productive, and unique level and are able to prove it false, not because it was put there to offend or to be, but because that means that you are thinking. I hope that when you do, you read on, not to find more, but because that is how relationships with humans go. You are bound to find one thing you love, one thing you hate, and five more that you may be completely indifferent to, but at least you found love.

Data And Statistics

I love data and am fortunate to live in a time when I can look up any question and be met with numerous studies that can tell me the answer with numerical certainty. The problem with these numerous studies is that they are all different and the devil is in the details. All the data points have pages of study notes on how the numbers were arrived at, all the inconsistencies, outliers, sample information, and conflicting points. The fact is that no single statistic stated in narrow terms should be trusted.

If the presentation is not enough to distrust a statistic, the reason it exists may be. There are a potentially infinite number of groups that publish studies aimed at answering a question in a favorable way for corporations to sell products. This flood of what appears to be data is often purposefully misrepresented to fit narratives. If I want a statistic to prove that something is factually plausible, a simple internet search can help me with that.

    This is why I encourage you not to quote any statistic in this book. Numbers help us visualize the prevalence of an outcome. Some data in this book is the best published information on record, and some is directly from world governments, but as mentioned, it can all be manipulated. I hope that you can use this book to see data and check it against your experience. If you think a piece of data is radically incorrect, use that as a chance to look it up. Expand your knowledge and recontextualize the content in light of the updated numbers. Does the argument still hold? Unless you are a scientist or statistician, chances are that the methods of generating such data may escape the average person. I encourage us all not to base our opinions on information we are fed, but on how that information aligns with our understanding of the world. Build a solid framework of approximate truth, backed up by data, and used with extreme skepticism. We don't have to be right, we just have to think and be able to see bold lies.

Summary

This book is dedicated to my daughters and to my siblings. This book is for young people looking for answers to how to live a good life as an average person and to begin to think about the decisions they face in an economic fashion. I hope that if this is the first time that you are hearing about these basic financial principles, you can learn how they affect you literally and metaphorically. Most of all, I hope that this helps guide you through hard times and may even help you avoid some.

There is plenty wrong in the world, but there is plenty right about it, too. There is some information that previous generations possessed that we seem to have lost. Maybe they didn't know how to tell us, or maybe we didn't pay attention. We most likely thought we knew more, as all young people do. Ask your elders how they would handle the problems that you face. The answers may surprise you, and they may not be helpful at all, but ask. You never know when it will be your last chance to ask. Not all of them will write a book about it.

Life of Compounding Interest

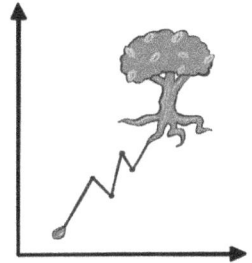

LIFE IS SIMPLY GROWING A PORTFOLIO

Albert Einstein has been credited with saying that "compound interest is the eighth wonder of the world." I have always found that to be fascinating. Not so much the quote itself, but who said it. This is arguably one of the greatest physicists of all time. Mathematics, physics, and the theory of relativity were his life. The calculations of annual rates of return or even the projections of a retirement portfolio would have been elementary from a mathematical perspective. No, it is clear that it isn't the math involved or even the concepts, but the vastness of what makes it work. For compounding interest to truly work, it requires many different aspects of life, economics, politics, time, and luck to work together in an intricate and delicate ecosystem to produce a beauty akin to an orchestra performance, available to anyone who wants to hear it.

Imagine, if you will, that you are required to sit and listen to Beethoven's Symphony 7. Now, a professional orchestra playing such a timeless and historic piece in this century is not going to be everyone's preference for music. While most would agree it is beautiful, it takes a certain level of familiarity with the craft to truly appreciate it. It is not lyrically relatable, it doesn't put off many intended vibes for others to pick up on, and it is made for you to experience in your own unique way. The feelings, memories, and emotions that such a moving piece of music is going to evoke, if you let it, are truly unique to you, even if similar to others. Someone describing the piece may resonate on some level, and you may be able to empathize with the sentiments and imprint them into your experience, but it still won't be exactly the same.

    Life and investing work the same way. Your experience truly is our own. You must experience life, like it or not; it is beautiful in its own way, and it's all yours. How you experience life will be subject to the exposures, experiences, interests, knowledge, decisions, and appreciations. There are some out there who will simply not appreciate life at all, seeing it as oppressive and pointless. There is an infinite number of exposures and experiences an individual will have in our complex world, and that means that there is no easy, one-size-fits-all plan or path to success. Even a definition of success is unique to the individual.

    Aside from the fact that "all the living must experience life," one order of business that plagues the last few generations in the West more than other times throughout history is the idea of financial security and retirement. If nothing else, this is due to the nuanced definitions. Security today encompasses so much more than fear of hunger and inadequate shelter, and the concept of retirement is relatively new. Retirement, in all this, is simply the accumulation of all the efforts and discipline that one has applied throughout their life. It is where the fruits of sacrifice, education, work, savings, investments, risks, and luck shake out to produce the level of financial stability you will experience for the final twenty to thirty percent of your life. The tree from which that fruit falls is difficult to grow, and frankly, it isn't very fun. About as much fun as watching trees grow. It is also work, literally. Researching, planning, saving, and monitoring in the complex investing landscape is as long and arduous as your career will be, with ups and downs all the way. Undoubtedly, that is one of the many driving forces behind the worrying statistics on the American savings rate in the last few generations. Statistics such as more than a quarter of Americans couldn't afford a one-thousand dollar emergency, nearly eighty percent of people believe that they won't have enough saved to retire, and the median retirement account balance for those age sixty four has been reported at less than two hundred thousand when they should be at their highest, with enough to sustain them for twenty or more years.

    We have done a lot of work to perfect the hedonistic treadmill while simultaneously shortening our attention span to short-term goals. The idea that we may live forever and there is always more time may be closer to true than ever, thanks to modern science, but we rarely stop to truly reflect on what that may look like and what kind of security we are forgoing in the future from the lack of discipline today.

    For all of human history, security has never been certain or expected. That is part of the human experience. Over a millennium ago, the Buddha was paraphrased as saying, "life is suffering," and a large part of the religion's faith is attributed to managing that first Noble Truth. At some time in everyone's life, security will be a luxury that they cannot afford. Insecurity can be found in many forms. Obviously, one can experience financial insecurity, but it can also be from family, close relationships, health, or existential. These pieces of life that are critical to a person's level of security can be shaken to the core in trying times. These are the times when "an ounce of prevention is worth a pound of cure." These times are when it is imperative to have reserves squirreled away in each of these areas to account for the deficit that will inevitably occur. As part of life, you will likely lose a job, lose a loved one, get sick in some way, or question all you once believed. When that happens, the best you can hope for is that the preventative measures you invested in each of these areas will bolster you into the fastest recovery possible and help you see the possibilities that setbacks can present. Such hard times should not be gravely feared. The same "you only live once" mentality that can hinder your future stability if you only focus on short-term pleasure is the same mentality that can be used to plan your life to embody pleasure and have gratitude, as well as opportunity, when things don't go as easily as you may hope.

  This is why a common piece of investing advice that you will often hear is that a crash in the market is the best time to invest. The idea here is that when stocks are at their lowest price and you expect things to return to normal or better, as they often do, the calm and educated investor has a chance to yield the highest returns, especially in the short to medium term. The outcome we should all aim for is steady investment and somewhat predictable returns. However, investors know that the market will sometimes open a door for high rewards for those who are diligent and optimistic. The same principle works in life. Oftentimes at our lowest, we are given a chance to reset, regroup, and reprioritize. If you have been diligent in maintaining your reserves and are optimistic for better times, you will have a chance for increased returns.

So why the comparison between a life well-lived and financial principles? Why bother with comparing life to investing our money, and why should we think of our lives in terms of retiring? In short, it's all about making good, consistent, ongoing investments, managing our resources well, and proper goal setting. The currencies for retirement and a good life are different, but share many of the same principles and goals. Money is easy. It has rules, laws, and best practices. Life is a little messier. It has many currencies that trade at different values at different times. The things that make up your social capital will rightfully be different between family, friends, career, communities, and networks. However, the ultimate currency is that which we trade with our past, present, and future selves.

Retirement planning and wealth growth strategies are all about making the right choices that align with specified goals. These plans, if done right, should have flexibility and contingencies. There is an impossible amount of data and information about past performance, current market statistics, and predictions for the future for you to educate yourself with in hopes of making informed decisions for your future well-being. The way you apply this information will set your plan apart from others, for better or worse. There will not be a retirement plan exactly like yours, nor will any others yield the same results. Sound familiar in concept? Much like no one's life experience will be the same as yours, neither will your goals or approach. These unique aspects drive your decisions and help manage all the ups and downs.

To retirement specifically, it is an end state for wealth accumulation. If we ever hope to graduate to a phase in life away from the requirement of working to pay the bills, it requires investing and intentionality. Without a plan to move to the retirement phase, you will almost certainly never hit it. Those without such plans risk the need to exchange time for resources cyclically until they run out of both, at which time they must surrender to the mercy of others for necessities and their quality of life. Removing a person's autonomy or the ability to acquire their most basic needs and desires cripples the human spirit. Furthermore, relying on charity requires charitable acts from others. The line between pity and charity is thin. Relying on others for these needs runs a risk of dissolving strong and respected bonds. I believe that we all want to move through life continuously adding our unique value to our communities and leave legacies of ourselves in their fullest form. I hope and wish for everyone the ability to maintain independence and dignity as long as possible. To which I only suggest that we aim to live a life 'in the black,' regardless of the currency you trade in.

    The idea of retirement has also evolved as much as any other aspect in our world within the last fifty years. For example, most of our great-grandparents who worked between 1950 and 1975 likely had some sort of inherent retirement savings that saved them from needing to contribute large amounts of their wages towards retirement. In America, according to a bulletin from the US Social Security administration in 1969, forty-eight percent of workers had employer-managed pension options.[1] Contribution benchmarks at this time were only three and a half percent. So, on average, less than four percent of our grandparents' wages needed to go to retirement savings, whereas today, best practice is ten percent or more. In addition, they received social security benefits to the fullest extent when considering disbursements and inflation. I am not suggesting that this generation collected lavish sums from these benefits. However, these benefits in many cases kept them above the poverty line for single or two-member households, as many retirees in the US are. Most importantly, it was a consistent stream of income that one could simply expect as a working citizen.

Before this golden age of pensions, family was the retirement plan. It was very socially acceptable that children could care for aging parents, and multigenerational households were commonplace. Couples with multiple children had options, and expenses could be much more evenly distributed. Life expectancies were generally shorter as well. Undoubtedly, this was a different time with different priorities and standards of living. Life was simpler in a way with a much smaller number of *necessary* expenses. Medical care was more basic and affordable, and the housing market allowed many more to own homes, part of which can be attributed to their smaller nature compared to the average home size today. Nonetheless, the principles were still the same. We all age and cannot work forever. We should all plan the best we can to account for that and have the minimal negative impact following this life transition, because life is not that simple anymore, and the safety nets that once were common are not going to save anyone after the baby boomer generation.

With the changes to our societal and financial landscapes, it is critical that we update our strategies where needed, not only for the material world as we learn to navigate new economic challenges, but also for the ways that we traverse the new normals that society adopts. We have to strongly advocate for the fact that the human condition remains the same to a large extent. We are all still here, trying to find our place, trying to leave our mark, and trying to do the best we can to be content with ourselves. We have thousands of years' worth of life lessons, whether you cling to philosophy, science, or religion. Many of these have the most basic foundations set in stone for us to cling to, regardless of nuances. We know what is good, we know what makes us truly happy, and we know that we hold a unique value. The goals are the same, though the obstacles and rules can change. Let's, rather than arguing over changing landscapes with others and ourselves, keep our eye on the goal and stay focused on what we know worked for the people that came before us, apply those principles to our current world, and pave a way for our future selves to experience a full and wealthy life.

Perception frames everything, and in our society today, our perception is derived from those around us. We constantly take in signals of success from those around us and use them to measure our own. This is very natural and ingrained in us at an evolutionary level. We need to see what the rest of the tribe is doing and doing well to integrate and thrive collectively. Harmless enough. Today, we are bombarded with material signs of success and rarely see what is happening under the hood. Large houses and lavish vacations are posted with airbrushed and filtered physiques. We bring our most positive moods to work and signal competence and cool under pressure. This is what the culture feeds us as wealth and success. Sadly, these material signals speak very little to happiness, impact, or health in our personal, financial, and work lives, serving as a poor metric to gauge lifelong success.

There is a saying in personal finance, "If you do what everyone else is doing, you will likely end up with the same results." Normally, this is said to point out that most people work too hard at a job they hate, to buy things they do not need, to impress people they do not even like. You can easily spin this mentality, though, to focus on "average actions produce average results." Sounds underwhelming, but it could possibly be the most empowering thing you could take to heart. I hate to break it to all those who feel exceptional, but statistically speaking, you are likely very average. Eighty percent of us fall in the middle of most bell curves, from intelligence to talent and even wealth. It's not exciting or uplifting if you hope for others to see you as exceptionally unique and uncategorizable, but if you were to find yourself as a data point in a series of graphs, that is just the reality. Even if you exceed average in an area, you may find yourself in the lowest distribution in other areas. What is uplifting is that you have an amazing opportunity if you can internalize this label. By being so average, you have all the statistics of realistic probability at your fingertips, and more case studies will apply to you, more than any outliers. You can gauge with confidence your earning potential, a conservative portfolio's expected growth over time, average retirement age, and all the way to the likelihood of marital and parental outcomes, along with all the applicable tips and tricks to make these things happen for the average individual. It is amazing the information catered to the average person if you are willing to lump yourself into the title of average. Even more to these numbers and to garner some appreciation from Western readers, the average wages in the US were around sixty thousand dollars in 2024.[2] That average US salary puts you in roughly the top one percent of the world.[3] Lastly, an often quoted survey by Ramsey Solutions of US millionaires, that is, people who have more than a million dollars in liquid assets, only thirty-one percent of those surveyed averaged more than one hundred thousand dollars annually through their career, and roughly a third of all respondents never hit the six-figure mark.[4] Removing your visual cues of wealth from your neighbors, being average is not looking so bad.

Finding meaning and happiness in life is the oldest philosophical question and dilemma, going back before the works of Socrates. I would not dare place my knowledge against theirs or claim to have better solutions. However, I can say that I have found applying economic models to how I plan and conduct myself, not to find meaning necessarily, but to give purpose and consistency to my decision-making. I attempt to, rather than make the best decisions, prevent myself from making the worst choices. Sometimes that is all we need to keep moving; small steps that propel us in a positive direction and a north star to guide us through inevitable setbacks. While everyone's definitions of security will vary, it is one of the foundational drivers that sits at the base of Maslow's hierarchy of needs, trumped only by the very sustenance that keeps us biologically functioning. That is because food keeps us physically functioning as an animal, but security gives us the sustenance needed to function as a person and the space to progress past the next meal.

There are so many things in life where you only get one chance, but in the world of investing, you have a chance to adjust, correct, and still hit goals. Investing for retirement should be designed to compensate for all stages of life and must be catered to the individual. No two plans or portfolios will be alike. It requires knowledge and assistance, planning and discipline, pessimism and optimism for the future, but most importantly, conscious and continuous effort towards an inevitable and uniquely human end - aging gracefully at every stage with security and self-assuredness.

Life is Simply Growing a Portfolio

The concept of capital essence

While money is the metric to gauge our financial and material success, it does a poor job of gauging non-monetary success. It is absolutely possible to live a full, happy, productive, and overall successful life without amassing large sums of wealth or living lavishly. In reality, more people achieve this than those who end their lives materially rich. Humble lives have as much or more potential to generate true happiness and contentment while leaving lasting, positive impressions on their corner of the world.

Therefore, to detach from monetary scorekeeping, a concept that I would like to present to gauge success and non-material wealth accumulation, is Capital Essence. This concept aims to help view life and efforts in economic terms, going beyond simply money. Capital Essence can be thought of as the value of what you intangibly acquire to sustain you. It is essentially the currency that you are saving against to fill your portfolio and withdraw as needed.

Imagine how you see the amount in your bank account, and rather than a dollar sign, the sign of the currency is the image of you. If you were to have a scorecard that you used to gauge success in life, the goal you save towards, or the metric you chase to feel your sacrifices are worth it, that is your Capital Essence. Your accumulation of Capital Essence is independent of your material wealth. It can be earned, used to acquire certain things, and its accumulation is measurable. It can also be seen by others as a status symbol.

It is important we understand what capital is first, as well as its elements that expand far beyond simplistic comparisons to dollars and cents. In economic terms, capital is physical or financial resources used to create value in an economy. That is fairly simple and broad, no doubt. However, all the elements of investing, economic and personal, lie in that definition.

Physical resources are your tangibles. These could be your house if you own it, or it could be your time. They are things that have a direct value, can appreciate and depreciate, and are subject to direct trade. The value is defined, more or less, by what others are willing to pay for it and is deeply entrenched in the laws of supply and demand.

Financial assets are a bit more complex and involved, and one of the highest classes of financial assets is currency. Let's start with the basics of trade. All trade starts with the concept of bartering. Let's say you make bread and I raise chickens for eggs. You eat bread every day and would like some eggs. I eat eggs every day and would like some bread. We can exchange our goods. Agree on a rate, say twelve eggs for a loaf of bread, and trade. This is mutually beneficial and easy. Let's say another person wants bread, but doesn't have anything to trade. They are willing to offer a day's labor for a loaf of bread. If they don't need help, there is no reason to trade. If I need some help and am willing to offer a dozen eggs for a day's work, that person could then trade the dozen eggs to you for a loaf of bread, and everything works out.

This is the heart of basic monetary function. Rather than bartering amongst each other to get what we need, money now serves as the unifying bartering item. In that example, a day's work, a loaf of bread, and a dozen eggs have an agreed-upon equal value amongst those trading. Introduce money into the equation, and that agreed-upon value could be one dollar. That one dollar is based on the local markets for goods. What people need and what people have.

If you live in one region, corn may be plentiful and potatoes scarce, and the opposite in a neighboring region. In the first region, corn is cheap and potatoes are expensive due to the supply and demand. It only makes sense to trade with a partner that has a need for your cheap corn and is looking to offload their cheap potatoes. Again, everyone wins by supplying people with the best balance of goods for the best price, enriching everyone's life. The basis of the trading relationship is the ability to consistently produce what we are best at producing while maintaining some demand for other products to trade for. While corn and potatoes are still tangible goods, they are the sole means of trade and our single source of economic value, making these commodities less of a physical resource and more of a currency.

Currency is the governing means of trade, generally within a single country. The distribution, value, and management of it are primarily a function of a nation's governing body. The value of a currency could be seen as relative. While inside the currency's home country's borders as a means of trade, the value is relatively constant. To say one dollar equals one dollar, and we don't think much about it past that. The value to the rest of the world is a much different case. All of a sudden, the value of your dollar becomes relative to where you are trading. Your currency now needs an international value to assess its buying power in the economy where the purchase is taking place. Your one US Dollar could equal seventeen Mexican Pesos or one hundred forty Japanese Yen, all with their relative value to that same good. Then there is the cost of exchange. Changing your currencies as a consumer will cost you to convert your native currency into a foreign one. Because there is a cost and benefit in holding other currencies, depending on where they stand in the world's marketplace, these exchange rates are based on a myriad of metrics, but most rely on how things are going in that country economically, the country's stability, quantity of currency, and relations with trading countries.

While it has dissolved as a monetary policy worldwide, like the US, there was something called the gold standard. Put simply, the gold standard is a system where gold is the true central currency. A country's currency was measured in a unit of gold. To say, a single ounce of gold may cost one hundred US Dollars, seven hundred Mexican Pesos, or eighty-five British Pounds. This gold standard helped unify currency value based on a single asset and gave all countries an alternative currency to trade in that was universally accepted. Simpler times.

Capital Essence is the Capital someone trades with themselves. Every person possesses their own capital. Physical assets like time, attention, and energy are finite in nature and carry a unique value. While they can be given or traded, their value is subject to supply and demand. Likewise, everyone operates their

The Concept Of Capital Essence

own currency. They control the distribution, monitor inflation, and do what they can to maximize its value to others they hope to trade with. Not everyone's currency is worth the same, and tariffs will exist on certain goods among partners, but all will have unique value propositions and hold a place in this vast economy we call society. However, the fact remains the same with currency- it is intended for trade within one's own borders.

There is still a gold standard in the world of your personal currency. There are unifying aspects that everyone trades in. This can be actual money or your value in the economy, because you must trade with others who are not interested in your personal value at some point. They won't check up on you when you are sick, nor come to you for advice. They are cold, but necessary transactions. These trading partners may be governments or corporations. They will assign a value to you and act accordingly. While they may not be invested in your success, they certainly can influence it. You have to hold some amount of this common currency and be able to operate within its regulations. Yes, you have to cooperate with the world and cannot separate from it. Money and real-world economic viability are important, just as it is being a functional citizen. Whatever amount of your personal currency you amass, at some point, it will be weighed against the world's common exchange rates.

Still, your capital essence must be managed like any economy. You can control the aspects of what your currency and trade are worth. Share yourself too much or too easily with the world, and you can dilute your currency. Don't participate enough in trading currencies with others, and you create scarcity. Trade with others dishonestly or in a predatory manner, and you will lower trust. Don't produce things people can come to you uniquely for, and there is no trade at all. For the good and bad, what you can and do offer defines your worth.

Since you are trading within your sovereign borders, your currency is king. Your currency flows easiest within your scope of rule. Your trade policies and the costs within you can be managed more easily than anywhere outside yourself, so you have control to put your interests above others, and you must to some great extent.

You are not simply acting in the interest of your current self; you need to be strategic and set your future self up for success. Like every parent should hope for a better life for their offspring, we too need to hope for a better life for our future selves. We want our currency to be worth as much as possible and to allow easy exchange with others. Maximizing our trading potential is ideal in all aspects of life if we hope to be able to trade our expertise for others', creating a whole and prosperous existence.

While you are managing your currency and its value, you must also manage how much you keep for yourself in reserves. You must squirrel away spending power to maintain your own independence, sovereignty, and relevance. To do this, you start to maintain a level of capital to pay your own bills, now and in the future. It's a bank account that you cannot allow to be depleted. Sometimes you will have surplus periods and sometimes deficits, but like any portfolio, it will grow over time if given long enough in the market. The bills that you are responsible for are more than power and water; they are also the knowledge, experience, and motivation to maintain a healthy and stable life. The very will to keep going.

While understanding your personal currency is extremely important so that you may apply its principles in understanding value, cost-benefit analysis, and trade, Capital Essence in practice encompasses much more. It is made up of all your economic viability. Not simply your material wealth accumulation, though. Your ability to accumulate money may be part of it, but not all of it. It is your competence, your network, your reputation, your accessibility, your capacity for love and empathy. All the things that make life worth living and make you someone others want to be in the company of. It is the acts and investments that you made in life that draw people to pay their respects at your funeral and support your loved ones when you are gone. It is the value that you gave to others that leads them to assist you enthusiastically in your moment of need. It is also the reputation you have that makes people want to ask your advice or opinions and value your input.

Let's say you have three friends. One who works a dead-end job with no motivation to excel. They have no partner, are minimally involved with their family and community, and spend most of their time out of work playing video games, watching TV, and fully immersed in niche hobbies. The second friend is relatively successful in sales. They are always the life of the party, and not always in a good way. Their relationships are rife with drama, and they struggle with substance abuse. The third friend has a successful career that they love and continue to be promoted. They don't go out very much because they have a family they are devoted to, and their family life is stable and healthy. Now, all three of these friends may bring something uniquely valuable to the relationship and have plenty of reasons to remain friends. You may have known each other for a long time, they may have helped you in the past, or you simply have a good time when you are with them. Again, they are your friends for a reason.

The Concept Of Capital Essence

One day, you have a problem. Maybe you are struggling with something, are sick and need help, have some amazing news to share, or simply need advice. What friend is likely going to be the one you turn to? The first friend probably is not equipped to offer sound advice, understand your position, or be of much use. The second friend may be of some help and ready to come to your aid, but is not known for being reliable or sympathetic. They'll likely try to one-up your good news or offer trite or bad advice. The third friend may be busy, but they likely could see a friend in need and carve out some time because they know what is important. Their advice will likely come from a place of empathy, care, and experience. They are not in competition with you, so when you tell them good news, they are genuinely excited. The third friend is likely the preferred choice of who you would want by your side in tough times.

This is a demonstration of a higher accumulation of capital essence. Others notice the ability to make good decisions, act with a level of care, and be of use when called upon. This type of recognition is an honor that is earned. The kind that compounds. When people like working with you, they open doors for you. When you have been there for people, they feel indebted and want to pay you back for your kindness. When you gain experience and success in any aspect of life, others wish to follow you. This is what living a good life achieves: connection, admiration, and growth. It achieves a higher level of success than any one aspect alone could and propels you to raise others up with you.

This idea of your personal capital essence is growing your wealth in a currency that is yours and yours alone. The value of the assets you accumulate utilizing your innate assets is what you will survive, and hopefully thrive, on in the later phases of life. Life is something of a balance sheet. You can spend more than you have today, but your future self is who will pay. So avoid debt, fill your account, collect the interest and dividends, and live a comfortable life capable of sharing your wealth with others.

You are your own business

We like to see and think of ourselves as individuals. Unique human beings with intrinsic value apart from what we produce. Some part of us is that unique, valuable human being and worthy of all the human rights fought for and established in the last few centuries. It is also very common and easy to see ourselves as the hero in our stories and others that we share the world with as the Non-Playable Characters or "NPCs," akin to the spectators in video games with no mission or autonomy. Those around us are something of a mystery. We do not know what is going on in their thoughts, so we can't control or predict them. Oftentimes, their actions seem not to affect us at all, so their role in your journey is minimal. This is also the same mentality that leads us to feel that everyone else has things much more figured out than us. The same experience of not being able to see someone else's full story, mixed with good manners of trying to put one's best foot forward, is also what creates the facade of togetherness in others, seeing only what they want us to see. Everyone needs to uphold this image of competence and confidence because that is what leads us to be invited, accepted, and allowed to participate in some of the more exclusive parts of life, like friendship or employment. Ever feel that pull to show that you have it all together? Maybe you are so used to putting your best foot forward that it seems normal, and you don't even notice it.

There are a few terms that have become commonplace, overused, and misused recently, as most things in public spaces focus on inclusiveness and lowering tolerances for behavior that acts in self-interest. The first is narcissism. It seems like most of our exes could easily be written off as narcissists, and you could absolve yourself of any potential need for explanation or guilt in breaking things off. Narcissism is simply defined as a person who has an excessive interest in or admiration of themselves. From that definition alone, remove the word "excessive" and you have a healthy, self-confident person. At its extremes, it may warrant a diagnosis of Narcissistic Personality Disorder. At these extremes, people exhibit unhealthy amounts of vanity and selfishness, causing issues in relationships and work. Many studies estimate that the percentage of the population with this disorder is about five percent, but some studies have it as high as fifteen percent in the US.[5]

The other label that flies around in conversation too casually is sociopath. A bit more extreme than narcissism, warranting the category of pathology, sociopathy is a mental health condition in which a person consistently shows no regard for right and wrong and ignores the rights and feelings of others. Where a narcissist is more likely to feel they deserve special treatment when acting selfishly, a sociopath is more likely to lie, cheat, and steal to attain what they want. As our society has grown, expanded to more impersonal modes of business and communication, and begun to experience more prosperity, sociopathic behavior has become more tolerated and even expected. Ever find yourself more understanding of such bad behavior? Well, you see it more than ever in the media, both in the real world and in acts of fiction. Sociopathy or Antisocial Personality Disorder is only estimated to be experienced by one to four percent of people and is most prevalent in your twenties to forties, yet it seems that the label is applied much more frequently.[6] I believe the key word in the definition here is "consistency." Everyone lies, cheats, and steals at some time for some reason. That does not make us all sociopaths; it simply makes us social creatures, seeking admiration and acceptance. Sometimes we just try to take shortcuts.

So why even bring this up? Well, we need some of these aspects in our lives to align ourselves correctly and frame our decision-making. We all need a healthy level of narcissistic behavior to make decisions in our self-interest, and we need to know that even a spree of bad behavior doesn't warrant landing us a clinical diagnosis of a demonized personality trait. Self-promotion is something that we should all do to communicate our competencies. Furthermore, while lying should not be a habit to fall into, a white lie or withholding some information to protect someone's feelings or promote smooth social interactions is arguably the more accepted and humane way to go, rather than pummeling people with blunt or rude honesty. We need these aspects to think economically and a few steps ahead, beyond the first-level consequences of our decisions, to the best sustainable outcomes.

One of the best ways to embody these practices of healthily

advocating for self-interest and overall economic thinking is to imagine yourself as a business and operate accordingly as a manager. This shouldn't remove your individuality. After all, businesses can have personalities, multiple product lines, and even research and development functions to diversify and innovate. What businesses have that we don't normally is the obligation to hold ourselves to our missions and accounting departments. The mission, no matter what cute mission statement a company maintains for its employees to attempt to attribute some bigger meaning to their work, is to make money. To make money in a sustained fashion. To do that, it requires marketing, sales, support, operations, accounting, and people management functions. All these functions contribute to the mission of bringing in more money than is being spent in a long-term fashion.

In the spirit of imagining yourself as a business, the biggest thing to remember is that you are the product. You have something unique to offer the world, and that brings the challenge of how to define and present yourself. This is not about being flashy or the next big thing; it is about finding the best fit. There are millions of businesses in this world that are necessary, profitable, and not at all glamorous. For every revolutionary tech device, there is a manufacturer of the cords. For every house built, there has to be a nail manufacturer. Just like for every bit of food you eat, there was a farmer to grow it or a driver to transport it. Sometimes the smaller pieces or functions do not get the time in the spotlight, but they are invaluable to the offering. They are profitable and necessary businesses that rely on sales and the quality of the product or service delivered. Your product may never be what people think of buying, but you certainly have a critical role to play in the process.

Do not limit your offerings to glamorous titles. Build your product around the needs of customers and your strengths and experiences.

Sales are key to any successful business. To sell a product or service, you have to have some confidence in it. Enough confidence and knowledge to deliver concisely the benefits of purchasing your wares versus any of the competitors in the market. You have to use this confidence and knowledge to build enough of a trusted relationship that your prospective customer will be willing to give you their money. Lastly, to start that conversation and close that sale, it takes understanding of the problem you are trying to solve. There is an old saying in sales that people don't buy products, they buy solutions to their problems. To understand and empathize with prospective customers, it takes listening with genuine interest. It takes understanding the market and finding out where your strengths lie and how you can leverage them to fit needs and solve problems. Because at the end of the day, you should not be convincing people to buy anything as a salesperson; you are simply helping them realize how your product is the best fit for their needs.

Sales and marketing are not the same thing. While sales facilitates the transaction and serves to consult on specific questions, marketing gets a company's name out there and generates awareness. Marketing has three key elements: Product, Placement, and Promotion. The product in marketing is ensuring the fit for the needs. Again, understanding the application to maximize the likelihood of being a good fit for customer needs. Placement is ensuring that the product is in the right place to be seen at just the right time, whether that is distribution, displays, or sales locations. Lastly, there is a promotion: what most people think of when it comes to marketing. Promoting a product is about ensuring awareness of the product and company. While advertisements are a part of this, it is mostly about creating compelling points of engagement to generate knowledge and interest to be activated when a need for that product presents itself.

The most important aspect of promotion is brand. This is the product's holistic presentation. Everything is wrapped up in a unique personality. This should be a consistent set of messages and images that help customers feel familiar with a product offering and believe that they know what they are getting. In normal consumer goods, you will likely notice how the problem that the product solves, the packaging, the location in the stores, and the advertisements all work together to bring you a predictable experience. This is why brands call attention to new packaging or appearance. The old, "New Look, Same Great Taste" line. It is because they have to acknowledge that the product is still the predictable product that you are used to, and just looks different on the shelf. Novelty is great for a one-time purchase when you feel adventurous, but humans like a degree of certainty and want to interact more with people, places, and things they are familiar with. Branding builds that familiar relationship between people and the products they consume.

Product definition, sales pitches, and all the elements of marketing are key elements to functioning in society as people. It makes up your brand. You are constantly emitting signals of who you are, what you believe, what you do, and how you could solve problems for others. These problems do not have to be big ones. Sometimes the problem is just a stranger seeking some positive interaction with another human being. A predictable, "Hello, nice weather we're having," kind of interaction. Sometimes it could be an unspoken audition of character. Maybe this acquaintance could vouch for you to get a job or an introduction for a potential romantic partner. We constantly build our brand with people and are helping others quickly define us by how we present ourselves and act. That way, when a need arises for something you are associated with, you come to mind.

This all sounds relatively shallow, a bit dehumanizing, and impersonal. Thinking of yourself as a product to be peddled and called on by others when a need arises. That is the point, however. If you take all these personal aspects of putting yourself out there and getting to know or simply interacting with others, the process is predictable and transactional. In that transaction, you have the power to position yourself as needed for the situation. You have a chance to choose what advertisements others see, and evolve that message as time goes on. You do this subconsciously all the time when you talk to your best friend and boss differently, or when you tell your parents deep and personal insights of your day, and spare the cashier at a store that level of detail about your day. You are projecting a brand, you are letting them know what needs you are there to meet, and likewise. Why not start at an unemotional level and deepen the engagement further?

Like a business needs to get money from its customers to survive, we too need something from all the people we interact with. Love, acceptance, cooperation, companionship, time, help, and resources are things we all need and cannot provide for ourselves. In the same way that we have to trade and barter for all our physical needs, we do this for our emotional needs as well. All good relationships are symbiotic. Both sides are getting something out of ongoing participation, and likely not the same thing. Is it not better if you are upfront about what you bring to the table and what you seek in return? You will always have the off-menu items that you reserve for those you wish to invite in, but for most, they interact with you through your personal brand and offerings.

Acquiring and managing customers is only one side of a business, though. The back office operations are critical to running a successful business. At some point, if a business is not managed properly, it won't matter how many customers they acquire; if it costs more to run the business than it makes, it will fail. You have the same responsibilities to run your life in a way that you are making sound decisions to ensure that you are bringing in more than you spend. This requires thoughtful and efficient systems and processes to manage tasks like accounts payable and receivable, payroll, and administration, watching what is happening in daily operations, and monitoring the health of the organization. These are most easily defined as habits and routines. Whether it is how you treat your paycheck every week in regards to savings and budget, your morning and nighttime routines, how you care for your living space, or how you make and use your free time these habits keep things running and if one area goes awry, it has ripple effects across your life. Small inefficiencies or neglect may not be catastrophic, trust me, all businesses have some irrationally inefficient processes, but they do cost time, effort, and money.

Business problems normally have a relatively straightforward path to resolution. Someone on the payroll can take responsibility and problem-solve to alleviate the specific issue. For example, a business is having trouble properly tracking expenses and creating accurate expense breakdowns by the next quarter to create proper sales projections in the new year. Well, a new process around coding expenses should help identify where the money is going, so you can create and enforce the new policy. Will it be perfect, first try? Highly unlikely, but the overarching structure is in place, and adjustments can be made until it is fully dialed in and running smoothly, and the new information should help with the projections. Why not do the same in your life? You see, something is not working the way it should. Knowing what you want to work on better is the problem; identifying some step in the direction of improving it and acting on it will produce positive change. Maybe you never feel good about your house. You don't think it looks good, you aren't comfortable in it, and you never want to have anyone over. Make some effort to change it. Clean it, hang a picture, and add some light. Is it all better? Well, probably not, but that first step and the time spent can spark inspiration and the desire to finish the job. Like in business, give yourself a deadline. A realistic, but rapid deadline with a reason and a chance for feedback. Now that you have taken that first step, schedule someone to come over soon and use that pressure to push you to get the project to an acceptable place. The compliments on the changes will reinforce the value of the work you put in, and hopefully, you reap benefits from the more livable space in your alone time as well.

    Businesses make decisions to drive them towards their goals, chiefly it is to make more money and stay in business. All other goals will fall after the success of the business in those terms. When any business leader is making a decision on which direction to go, they are weighing the costs against the profits to be made. They are taking the risks into account to mitigate losses and managing all the key relationships with boards, investors, customers, and employees. They do this in a cold and calculated way that looks good on a spreadsheet or graph, removing emotion and presenting a logical argument for the decision. Everything we do and every decision we make is fundamentally the same. We have costs and benefits, risks, and other people to consider when it comes to protecting our own interests. There is always a better and worse choice that either benefits or hurts our future self. We so often let emotion, arbitrary obligation, and fear of effort influence our decisions and ultimately steer us in less than optimal directions. We have to play the long game and make the cold, calculated decisions if you do not want to look back with regret, because when you decide against what you know to be the better choice for feeling-based reasons, you will likely wish you had done it a little differently. It hurts to know that you had a better choice available and did not take it.

  Business has some built-in grace to its model, though. They look at reports on success periodically. Most businesses assess their success in quarterly and annual terms, and it isn't by accident. Bad quarters and even bad years will happen in the life of the business, but that can't be a perpetuating narrative. It is time to readjust expectations. You base next year's goals on this year's performance to show growth. You reset your targets each quarter to give yourself a reset and a short-term goal to aim for without having to hold the weight of the past, holding you back. Could you imagine judging a company's stock only by its starting value and today's value? That won't tell you anything useful unless you bought it on the first day, which is not the norm. Bitcoin would show a jump from ten cents in 2010 to a value of more than seventy thousand in 2024. Seven-hundred forty thousand percent looks a bit inflationary for anyone holding short-term bitcoin, and it removes the story of the large drops in 2014, 2019, and 2022. Success is not linear like that;

there are bad times in almost every success story, so we have to keep an eye on the short-term targets and recent history to maintain motivation to do the needed work today and save the long-term review for certain circumstances and periodical pats on the back for our growth. Furthermore, the decisions made to hit these quarterly and annual goals spark innovation and permanently alter the company. Likewise, your growth is on an upward trajectory, but it is not linear. You will have highs and lows on a daily basis, but you will learn and adapt to these circumstances, and you will permanently change and adapt to progress, leaving behind your old ways of doing things and evolving in ways to make your life run smoother and towards new priorities. Allow the change and embrace it. Trying to review your growth since birth is not useful for the next steps in your journey, but recent performance is. Keep the trophies from good times, but put the old ones in storage to make room for new ones on the shelf to remind yourself of your recent achievements towards today's goals.

Success, no matter how you define it, requires calculation, perseverance, and growth. It does not happen organically. Sometimes the success we obtain is not what we originally started off pursuing. Our definition of success changes over the years, as do we. One way to be mindful of these changes is to simply be present. It is tempting to set a distant future goal, some measurement of success, and grind towards it, sacrificing today for tomorrow. That is not necessarily a bad thing; in fact, it is great to keep a future self in mind and work towards a long-term consistent goal, but like a business, things have to be done today. Customers have to be served, money has to come in, and daily fires need to be managed and put out. Monitoring your short-term performance and adapting to the challenges of the day allows us to grow and focus. Our long-term goals provide motivation, but our short-term goals are steps, ensuring that we keep moving. No matter what grand plans we have, our primary goal is to stay in business and to be profitable. That necessity grounds us and keeps us in the present, trying to hit the goals for the month, the quarter, and the year. You are the business, after all. You are not the CEO, looking into the future and guiding the company towards long-term visions for success. You are not the salesperson trying to hit the monthly quota. You are not the accountant, making sure that you are prepared for the next audit. You are not the operations manager, just trying to make sure all the necessary tasks are done. These are all functions, necessary and important to manage if you want to be successful, but not the business. You can pivot the vision, you can have low sales months, and you can have faulty projections, but the business continues.

Making decisions with all those functions in mind is a collaborative business task. It requires some considerations for all the different aspects of the collective organization. If you place one function over another in terms of performance, you will strain the balance. Sacrifice financially sound decisions for sales, and you hurt the business. Setting wild goals without a plan of execution you hurt the business. You see these kinds of poor decisions being made like this every day in organizations, and it seems so obvious in hindsight. It is generally caused by a lack of consideration of all the complications involved in turning an idea into a reality in a complicated ecosystem, because not everyone can be in the room at once, and decisions have to be made. There is some cleanup that will always need to be done. The key is to make the cold, calculated best decision possible with the data available and the end in mind.

There is a concept of consequence order that breaks up the impact of decisions and actions. First-order consequences are the immediate feelings or results of the decision or action. Second-order consequences are the longer-term impacts of that action. Then, there are third-order consequences that are the longest-term impacts or true end result. Most decisions we make on a day-to-day basis focus only on the first-order consequence. If I do this, what is the immediate impact of this decision? This focuses on maximizing pleasure or minimizing pain when you break it down. In some ways, it is rational, but it isn't that forward-thinking. Second and third-order effects are not normally directly foreseeable either. They are achieved through a series of consecutive decisions stemming from the initial, compounding into the end result.

Let's say that you want to save money for the first time and you start contributing fifty dollars per week to a savings account. First-order consequences are that you will have about twenty-six hundred dollars after a year. Good job. You realize that you like the feeling of having that money in your savings account, it encourages you to contribute more, start investing to get some returns, and you develop the healthy habit of growing your wealth. All second-order consequences. For the third-order consequence, you likely have changed your life in an unimaginable way from the version of yourself that never started saving money. The benefits of developing that habit and mindset would rewire the way you think about money as a whole, changing your relationship to it entirely. The consecutive decisions that follow a simple habit of saving and wealth building are not measured only in the amount of money in an investment account, but the byproducts of security, confidence, and simple comfort around delayed gratification are life-changing.

Two people with the same upbringing and income, even the same job, will have a very different outlook and demeanor if one has significant savings versus spending everything that comes in. The stress levels alone of not having the financial security of savings in the event of an emergency will negatively alter behavior. The increased stress of full dependence on a scheduled paycheck can shift attitudes from relaxed and confident at work to anxious and fearful of messing up, in absolute fear of losing their job, crushing performance and advancement opportunities, and leading to overall dissatisfaction in the workplace. Everyone needs money, but the difference between paying expenses in cash with some buffer versus covering loans and fearing missing payments is stark.

In my experience, there are two sides to managing money, no matter your income. You manage the money you have, and the money you don't have manages you. This goes for people as well as businesses. Cash-solvent businesses operate much differently from investment-backed businesses. Venture capital is very prevalent in today's business world. Where investors loan a business money to build products and scale. This comes at the expense of ownership. To ensure the investors get returns on their investments, they get to help set earning expectations, and even have a seat at the table when it comes to decision-making on CEO tasks like company direction and operations. This makes maximizing profits at all costs the goal. Where companies that do not have these types of investors operate on their own profits to fund operations, they have full creative license on how their business is run. Often, this requires them to focus more on consistency and quality to maintain customers. They are more engaged in the people aspects of the business since relationships are their key to growth. Their reputation is paramount because their plan is to self-sustain and grow. The business isn't built simply to build a product and sell it off to larger entities as a planned exit strategy. In short, their success or failure is defined and executed on their terms for their people.

    That cash-solvent model is what we should be striving for in our lives. We acquire investors in many ways; family, friends, and romantic partners are easy ways to find yourself in some sort of social debt, and giving up decision-making power. This isn't always attributed to toxic relationships, but if you ask anything substantial of someone, they have something of a right to ensure they are getting their return on investment. If someone lends you money, they may have a right to ask what it is for, in ensuring that it isn't wasted, or even details on why you do not have the money. If nothing else, to have some faith that they will be repaid. If you need to move in with someone and you are not splitting all expenses and responsibilities equally, they have a claim to making rules to ensure they are not more inconvenienced by supporting you. Things like this have extremes, obviously, but the fact is that if you live in debt to others, you increase rules and restrictions on yourself. To fully enjoy independence and autonomy, you must maintain your self-sufficiency. In business and life, you have very little control over the environment you are in, even if you choose it. What you do have control over is how you operate in it. Sometimes you will want to take unconventional actions to increase happiness, well-being, and wealth. If you are indebted to others, you limit your creative potential and are expected to act predictably and conventionally conservative to maintain the relationship with those debtors. We all need help sometimes, but watch out for your debt, choose who you owe, know the terms, and try to minimize it all. Traveling lightly through this life is a form of wealth that money alone can't buy.

Thinking economically becomes easier when you think about things in business terms. When you know that your goal is simply to make money and stay in business as long as possible, decisions become simpler. Life is messy, and there is not always a scorecard or clear, better decisions. Separating yourself from you, the person, and you, the business, makes those decisions a little easier. Businesses do not care what the feelings are around business decisions aimed at increasing profits and adding long-term stability; that's just good business. Businesses know that if they lose vendors, partners, or customers that new ones can be found in the market. Is it easy, probably not, but the business must replace the function product they provided and move forward. Where life gets messy is currency. Most wealth in business is money. Life operates on a bit more. It is the culmination of time, effort, purpose, and resources that make up our capital essence. It still works the same. All decisions will have costs and benefits. If there is a cost, you should get some sort of benefit that exceeds the cost to be considered a viable trade. That is what enables growth for us and our wealth. The benefits to you may not be as simple as a quick payday. They could strengthen their relationships or their reputation. They could be reducing stress and adding time to your day, in which case, what you do with that time determines its worth. It could also be gaining skills and experience to make future tasks easier. Doing things to benefit yourself to these ends or not doing something because you cannot find what's in it for you does not make you toxic, narcissistic, or psychopathic. It makes you healthily self-interested and not willing to give away your resources without any return. It's just good business.

Economists found out a long time ago that people cannot be expected to act rationally in economic terms. The main reason is that the motivations are not always clear and logical. Emotions will generally produce unexpected and even counterproductive results because the goal changes from second and third order consequence reasoning to first order only, and minimizing discomfort or maximizing pleasure in the short-term. That is to say that emotional thinking blinds many to the downstream effects of their rash actions.

Having some level of control over these emotions as they relate to decision making, large and small, lays the groundwork for long-term success and minimizing regrets. Decision-making ability drives a person's success in all aspects of life, yet it seems like little time is spent honing this skill. The fastest way to start is to remember that you are a business and that requires cold and calculated decision-making as well as consideration for the entire organization and all its key functions. Having the ability to quickly assess at a high level the cost, payoff, and risk of decisions is invaluable once it becomes a habit. As economists could agree, rational decisions produce rational results. Knowing what the likely result of any decision is immediately reduces much of the anxiety of making that decision in the first place, because you have an idea of how it will turn out. You need to check with your analytics department and ensure they are constantly taking in relevant knowledge to produce good statistics and foresee risks, but as you acquire more information, decision-making gets easier and better.

You are the business. Your job is to maximize and sustain profits, regardless of the means. You get to evolve and adapt or even change entirely to meet this goal. Your metrics are focused on short-term and incremental performance towards your overall business goals. You must manage your functions internally and channel your inner C-suite leadership to manage all the various functions and interests that keep your business running efficiently. Most importantly, all this hinges on your ability to make good decisions. It feels like a long list of things to be done; it feels a lot like work. It is not a list, though; it's a mindset, and it's not work; it is a process. These are simply habits of looking at things in a particular way and framing your decision-making process around them. This mindset, if you can manage it, helps you in your career as employers look for this type of mindset in team members and leaders. It helps in your relationships, giving people a predictable experience and inherent boundaries. Most importantly, it focuses on forward and productive movement through life and helps limit stagnation on all fronts. It isn't selfish. You have to help yourself before you can help anyone. You give gifts, they are not stolen, nor are they required. Do not worry yourself with others not willing to offer enough value for your time or resources. Everyone wants something for free, but you have a business to run. This mentality helps safeguard all your most precious resources for things that offer value, because when we work together in life and business, we all lift each other up and progress together. Some businesses are small and some are large, but they all offer the same thing: a useful product to the market. Their customers are paying enough to generate some profit, regardless of how much. This is how business fundamentally has worked since commerce was introduced in prehistoric times, and it is hard-wired into our species. Capitalism has introduced complexities, scale, extremes, and its own issues, but the fact is that it is the rule of the land, and one person is not going to change this. That makes it where there are tons of resources to learn from and apply to your model, be it simple or complex. Learn, expand, and apply. Most importantly, practice good business, and it will pay off.

Take your assessments

When starting to invest for the first time, one common, first actionable step is to seek out a financial planner or advisor. These are people who live in the world of investing for long-term and practical purposes. They are not stockbrokers promising life-changing returns on investments. They don't make their money fast. But most importantly, their success hinges on yours. Are they for everyone? Well, no. Most of the knowledge they have access to can be easily found today. There are no barriers to setting up your entire investment strategy yourself. Many people find that to be too involved and risky, and the overwhelming effort to start things on their own paralyzes them into not starting at all. There are common practices, tax implications, as well as software and systems that financial advisers have knowledge of that, I feel, give me an edge as an early investor towards retirement. It still isn't without cost or risk, though. One risk and downside is the fees. The annual cost will be approximately one percent of your portfolio's worth. It doesn't sound like much, but as your account starts to grow, so do the fees. That one percent could potentially cost you about a quarter of your gains over the longevity of your retirement savings journey. The other is that many advisors are, in fact, salespeople, and if you do not know that and account for it, you will have a chance of making some bad investments for them to make commission.

There are generally two types of financial advisors. The first offers general financial advising services, but also provides an array of products that may have incentives tied to them for the financial advisor. There is nothing inherently wrong with this model if you trust the individual you are working with and do your due diligence to research the options. These financial planners will offer you many different paths to long-term success, and you may have a higher chance of stumbling into high-risk-high-reward options or very rigid commitments that you may not otherwise choose as part of a long-term strategy. It is important to know that most investment methods you will encounter in these settings fit some situation. Whole Life Insurance or Annuities will get a bad review from many financial influencers out there. They get that bad reputation when these products are sold to the wrong people and research wasn't done ahead of time, and they fail to follow the rules, but the truth is that they can present excellent strategic advantages when applied correctly and for the right people and circumstances. I will say those circumstances aren't terribly common.

The other type of financial advisor is a fiduciary. Fiduciaries hold additional certification distinctions that ensure that they are acting in the most transparent way possible and do not present any conflicts of interest when helping you make the best decision possible for your investments. Fiduciary duty implies that your well-being and benefit will come before their need for profit while under the care of their service. They will be the most transparent

Take Your Assessments

about their incentive structure and will likely charge a slightly higher fee to offset the revenue they lose from commissions. Yes, trust up front has a cost.

No matter which type of financial advisor you choose, you will receive guidance, education, assistance in setting up investment accounts, summaries, tax assistance, and regular reviews to track progress. This is what the fees are for. Any financial planner worth their salt will be completely ingrained in the success of their clients and ensure the best possible returns long-term. Even in tough markets, a financial planner who manages a portfolio that experiences losses will be under harsh scrutiny and risk losing swaths of customers. Being a successful financial planner is not easy. Eighty to ninety percent of financial planners who open a firm will close within five years. That means only as little as ten percent will have what it takes to build a client list and retain them long enough to sustain a living themselves. However, an established financial planner can generally expect a more than ninety percent retention rate of clients. This is meritocracy at its finest. The financial planning industry has no room for people who cannot attract clients with trust and retain them with results. When choosing your financial planner, seek experience.

All this is about financial planners and their benefits, and yet, according to the Northwestern Mutual Planning and Progress Study from 2022, only thirty-five percent of Americans use a financial planner.[7] There are likely many reasons why, starting with the dreaded statistics surrounding the fact that Americans just don't save money. According to a Motley Fool survey in 2023, seventy-one percent of Americans have five thousand dollars or less in savings, and forty-one percent have less than five hundred dollars.[8] Compare that with the average cost of car repair in 2022, coming in at three to four hundred dollars, and you can see there is not much of a buffer. Another reason is attributed to the democratization of financial services brought on by the internet and tech sectors, which makes the tasks associated with investing less of a hassle than previously. However, as good as the reasons are, a trusted financial planner is more than these services. They offer knowledge and insight that, if you are out earning your money to spend and save, you don't have time to acquire and validate. They offer the experience of working with many others, most likely, if you are just getting started, who are more experienced and successful. People who have seen their portfolio play out over the years and decades. They also offer the service of holding you accountable to your goals. Since their success hinges on yours, they need you to invest and have your portfolio grow. They take the sum of their knowledge and experience and help apply it to your unique situation and advocate for you to grow your wealth at every turn, wanting long-term security for you, and thus, for them.

Once you find your financial planner and walk into the first meeting, you will quickly notice that this is not a task to take lightly. You will divulge information that you may have never told anyone or even thought about yourself. The first job on this journey is an honest and thorough self-review. The important questions will center around your current situation, your potential, and your ambitions. From there, they can help you work backwards and set up a plan to meet those goals. To appropriately build a plan, they have to know what they are working with. They will ask what you do for a living, your level of education, your current assets, your current debt, your monthly expenses, when you want to retire, how much money you hope to have, and the list goes on. It does no one any service to lie here. Any misrepresentation of these aspects could completely alter the plan and its rate of success, so it is best to take true and honest stock of these items and lay them out in hopes of improving. I promise you, the number of people who walk into these first meetings, chest poked out, confident that they have it all figured out already, is small. It is hard to see the end in mind, having scoured the internet and knowing that you need a large sum of money set aside if you ever hope to escape the rat race, put your feet up, and finally have the security to leave the workforce. It is hard to realize that you may have made some mistakes financially before you ever thought about saving. All those twelve-dollar Starbucks runs now have a more bitter taste. I encourage you not to feel this way, sitting in your first meeting and assessing yourself. Remember, you have made the first step that sixty-five percent of Americans haven't made. Many are older, some in more need than you, but you took the initiative, not because you had it all figured out, but because you want to figure things out!

This anxiety doesn't have to be one you need to subject yourself to with proper thought. I advocate that you have answers to these questions long before you land in anyone's office, a financial advisor's, a hiring manager's, a pre-marriage counselor's, or a therapist's. These self-assessments are something that should be undergone early and regularly. Normally, by the age of sixteen, you have decisions immediately ahead of you that will start to shape the rest of your life. You will generally know just enough about yourself and the world to begin this type of assessment and start moving in the general direction you want to go. Despite what you may think, you won't know it all, though. You will not possess all the information you need to make the best decisions. Hell, your brain isn't even fully developed yet, and will have trouble processing the idea that you are only about 20% through your expected life.[9] It is a rare and critical time, though, when you can set yourself on a sure footing, ignoring any mistakes that have predated your planning phases, and they do not cause you the slightest loss in momentum. You can correct your educational mishaps, you can shed beliefs and habits that have held you back, and you can exert independence in your relationships. This isn't to suggest that you cannot and shouldn't do this at any other phases in life, or they will be any less effective, but self-discovery and goal setting done early and well provide a foundation that will influence effectiveness throughout life.

The first self-assessment factor is self-understanding. You will spend your entire life figuring this out and adapting to your own unconscious changes. However, you will be surprised to find that a large number of people in this world never actually take the time to get to know themselves in the early phases of life. They delegate a huge amount of this task to fleeting feelings, habits, and, worse, other people. When you are setting aside space to truly set your goals, it must be on your own, with as little comparison as possible. Forget that the rest of society exists for a bit and really think about yourself. Put yourself in the shoes of that financial advisor and ask yourself those tough questions. Think about yourself in the third person, as someone you are trying to get to know, and assess the situation before planning. Take stock of your current state, your potential, and what you truly want. Do this with no shame and be kind yet honest.

I challenge you to consider these things and believe them:

Take Your Assessments

You are not your experiences to date, you are not your habits, you are not what others see in you, and you are not the outcome of your efforts. You transcend all those things, and you are exactly who you are supposed to be. Your outcomes are heavily influenced by your actions, decisions, sacrifices, and honed abilities, but are also subject to a great deal of luck.

Issues will surely arise if you are not honest with yourself in your self-assessments. If you do not allot yourself some kindness, beating yourself up and demeaning yourself will surely corrupt the process. That negative voice is likely based on what you believe others think or have done and said, but defining yourself in terms of what others see will forfeit your very self and identity. You will lose yourself in the crowd and waste a lot of precious time trying to find yourself, walking in the paths of others. It is your journey after all, this life, so it's better to walk your own path and cherish when the paths of others merge with yours. Then you can go confidently together in the right direction or go your separate ways to your individual destinations.

Expectations can lead to a great deal of discontentment, but the true nemesis of happiness is an unachievable, critical goal. Expectations for your life that are not your own can never be met because these expectations lack the desires you truly seek to fulfill. Goals for yourself that you did not set will never achieve their desired outcomes, because goals lack meaning if you achieve the results you do not desire.

Other people can have expectations of you, and they likely will; you can exceed them, too. It is great if it works out that way, but failures to meet these expectations are equally as probable. You must know that any failure to meet others' expectations is not yours, but theirs. Not necessarily because their actions caused the goals and expectations not to be met, but because they attached such expectations to someone else. They looked to someone else to make something happen. Others can set rules and goals for you, and you can follow and exceed them, but the score, in the end, is theirs and not yours. Your score is one you have to keep from playing by your own rules. So set your own goals, mind your expectations, but be true to yourself in them. Your individuality is a blessing that comes at a cost, owning your outcomes. If you forego the cost, you will never see the blessing.

To start your goal setting, you will need to honestly assess yourself; you need to do it selfishly. In the beginning phases, remove all others from the thought experiments. These are your strengths; be proud of them. These are your weaknesses; acknowledge them. Other people can and should be part of your tactical and strategic goals, absolutely, but to look out for others, you have to first look out for yourself. Put on your oxygen mask before helping others, or get your own house in order before trying to correct the world. You are not going to be effective to your fullest potential if you are not able to self-sustain. More so, you will not be able to properly insert your true self and talents into the world if you are not properly oriented and aware of your capabilities. How do you orient yourself? Know your potential, your talents, and your limits so you can fully leverage them against the reality of the world you find yourself in. The goal is never about maximizing, but optimizing for your unique situation.

Assessing yourself can have limitless approaches and criteria to assess against. You can assess any aspect of yourself down to its deepest level. You can assess habits against your outcomes, or you can assess your behavior in the social feedback you receive. You are constantly doing this in your day-to-day life, whether you realize it or not. As you move through life, you will be assessing how things are and how you are fitting into them, from your level of inclusion, your performance, your behavior, and your outcomes. Assessing yourself consciously is a powerful habit because "you" are not something that is static. A shared superpower of our species is our ability to learn, adapt, grow, and change drastically as a result of our situations. These adaptations affect our personalities, abilities, and interests. Things or traits about us that, from an early age, we can identify so strongly with that we see as a part of our natural self can change. Who we think we are may fade away or intensify as our situations change. While some aspects of our personality we can keep with us through our entire life, and it is even thought that some personality traits could even be deeply hereditary, the way that we integrate those traits into our behavior can be fluid and changing. That integration of the traits guides us through our decision-making and helps make us predictable to ourselves. It helps us assess the future against our proclivities to predict and plan for the best achievable outcomes.

Assessing yourself is not easy. When wrestling with our own psychology, we like to think that we have a few tricks up our sleeves. We do not want to be predictable, because there are a lot of positive and cool factors attached to spontaneity. Being predictable feels monotonous and deterministic, threatening to take away our very ability to change. To some of us, the idea of dedication to a lifestyle, especially in the future, brings up feelings akin to claustrophobia. I encourage you not to let that fear come in. You are not assessing yourself against your future, but for it. You are not assessing yourself as a permanent being. No, you are assessing yourself as a growing and adapting human in a vast and complicated world. When assessing yourself, it is more of an inventory than a planning session.

As infants, a self-assessment would be pretty short. Your abilities are greatly limited. As you grow and progress into a toddler, you learn the skills that seem impossible if you are graded against your infant assessment. As an infant, you couldn't walk, but now you can. You couldn't talk, but you are starting to. At this stage, what you naturally won't pay attention to, due to the whole object permanence bit, is the steps that it took. You didn't just stand up and walk. You saw that other humans walked and got the idea that you needed to do that, you kicked thousands of times to build up strength to support yourself, you rolled and crawled to calibrate yourself for movement, you pulled up repeatedly to get used to the upright orientation, and then you took your first steps. None of this was necessarily conscious, but training, trial, and error to the habit of walking. An awesome thing about this, though, is that it was your goal and your timing; it was not imposed. Sure, you saw adults walk and thought that was the way to move. Your parents probably pushed the timeline and coached because they wanted you to walk, but without you, even as an infant desiring to take those steps, you would not. You were not worried about the developmental timing and milestones like your parents. You weren't comparing yourself to every other kid in the room in speed and technique. Those things are ingrained in us later in life. Your goals and motivations were pure. "I want to walk, so let me try and walk." Many of your goals and expectations in life are that way. Everyone else can be moving in a direction, and you can see that is a proper way to go; others can coach and push you to it, but taking that first step cannot happen with you being complicit in the action.

So, to start your assessment and orient yourself to answer the questions of "what are your goals and what paths you should take to get there," I suggest only a few items at a high level. Avoid the deep dives into all the facets of yourself and how you operate, not because it is not useful, but because we have two types of goals in life: the tactical and strategic. By definition and often described in business settings, strategic goals are the big end results; they are what we want to achieve over long periods of time and are, more or less, the destination. Tactical goals are the small goals that keep us moving in the direction that we want to go. Some will be the next step, some will be points far down the path, but tactical decisions are made as you execute effort towards your strategic goal. To ensure our focus remains on the Strategic, I suggest focusing primarily on these three aspects of self-assessment: Understanding, Ability, and Motivation.

Your understanding of the world or even yourself is far from opinions or basic facts. Our world, like ourselves, is vast, complicated, and evolving. No one has it all figured out. There are aspects of life and our physical world that we can study our entire lives and never fully grasp because of their complexity and their entanglement with other deep concepts and systems. Our existence is made up of symbiotic ecosystems in constant interaction with each other. This concept can expand all the way to time and space. Your career dream may be to understand our galaxy and beyond, but when assessing your understanding of your own life and its trajectory, you should probably bring your focus closer to the immediate task at hand.

The understanding I am speaking of is how the generalized

world works and how integrated you are in it. The twentieth century spun up technology at a faster rate than ever seen in history, and with it, advanced systems of standard operation. There was a time in the lives of many still with us when most things that we feel are necessities today may not have even existed. Many of the technological advances that we rely on are less than 40 years old and have also changed our lives in irreversible ways. It, in a sense, has changed the way we understand the world.

As recent as the 1990s, a common practice was to balance your checkbook. For those young enough to never have seen this done, a check was the first version of your debit card. A piece of paper containing your account information, written out to a specific amount for you to spend like cash. It would take a few days, but the person holding the check would give it to their bank, which would use it to transfer funds from your account to the check holder. Mundane and time-consuming, yes, but it was the manual steps to pay for anything without digital transfers. In the nineties, computers were used; before that, it was papers and phones. Before that, you likely didn't have the ability to write checks at all and relied solely on cash or bartering. When you balanced your checkbook, you were tracking the balance of your bank account against all the checks that you had out. By the way, before digital banking, you kept track of your own bank account balance. Sure, you could go to the bank or call for your balance, but that was timely, and you wanted to check their work as well. If you did not have the funds available when the check was to be cashed, it would bounce and your check would be worthless, leaving you on the hook to pay that amount as well as fees to all parties involved that treated your check as good through the process. This was an ecosystem that relied on the effort and trust of retailers, customers, and banks to keep functioning. If you didn't trust someone in that system, you wouldn't write or take checks. If anyone was not timely or detailed in their part of the process, money for everyone could be lost. Without basic knowledge of the process, though, you would likely be setting yourself up for failure when receiving your checkbook for the first time and subjecting yourself to the felony that is check fraud.

There are hundreds of systems like these that you need some understanding of simply to operate in the first world, more so if you aim to thrive. I have found that the more responsibility I take on, whether it is a new service I sign up for, new job roles, or starting a new type of investment, I expose myself to more of these systems. Are these systems efficient or even fair? Most definitely not. Every system that you subject yourself to, from your television subscription to your job, to your housing, all have overly complicated systems to provide something of value and protect the process in continuing to operate through profit and protection from losing it. They are rules and laws made up to keep the game going. You don't have much say in what the rules are, but if you are playing, you have to abide by them. If you understand them, then you can at least play to your fullest ability.

How these systems work in our society is in the contracts. If you are ever looking for a good scare, try reading most of the things you sign, look at the system you are agreeing to participate in, and consider how complicated it is. We don't read contracts most of time, though. All the rules are given to us to agree to, and we don't. If you have ever signed a contract in person, the person handing you the papers to sign will intuitively and maybe even unconsciously tell you what you are signing and their basic summary of it. Something like, "and if you miss a payment on your loan, this is where you are agreeing to the late fee structure." Funny thing is, many times they are oversimplifying or misrepresenting. Not normally out of malice, but they haven't read it, they weren't trained on it, and don't understand it themselves, and sitting quietly while you read a contract is socially excruciating.

Could you imagine that you are showing up to play baseball for the first time and you have never seen the game? The coach hands you the rule book and tells you that you have to stay in the locker room and read it before you come out to play. That is not how anyone has ever learned to play baseball. No, you watch, your coach tells you the basic rules for batting and fielding, and you hone the rules as you go. You don't generally question why you run counter-clockwise; you see people who have been playing longer and just do it. That is how most of us approach life and our economic participation: Watch, play, then check the rules if issues arise.

I suggest more of the board game approach. Almost everyone reading this would have played Monopoly before. To start, you have to read the rules. The board is less intuitive than a baseball field; there are more elements, and you know right away that there are special rules for the different spaces. You have to read how much money you get to start, when to roll the dice, and how the turn order goes. The rules tell you how to determine who wins and loses and how the process plays out with multiple players. Reading the rules before playing is a must and in many cases, understanding the rules can play into strategies and give you an upper hand in a game where everything starts equal and quickly shifts.

These systems aren't just the ones you opt into. You,

yourself, are one of these systems as well. Your personality, your tendencies, and even your limitations. It operates in its own ecosystem, heavily influenced by its environment. From the food you consume to the people you surround yourself with, your ecosystem is conditioned to the situations it is found in. Your system is wired up in its own special way, and understanding it is key to optimizing your expectations and overall growth. Optimization is the key. This is your system, and you have more input than any others in how it operates. You are your catalyst to change, but with that power in your hands, what should you change and what should you nurture?

To begin to figure it out, look at the actions and look at the ecosystems. How do you behave or react to certain situations and why? You likely have found yourself with certain people and in certain situations where you ask yourself, "Why did I behave that way?" Contrariwise, you may also have been in situations where you exceeded your expectations and thought, "How did I manage to achieve that?" This is where your system interacts with specific environments to bring out the best and worst in you. All too often, we find ourselves on autopilot and believing that we, our personalities, and abilities operate in a vacuum and our actions are completely and consciously our own. It is our system interacting with others, and that isn't always predictable. There are times in our lives when our systems are mature and steadfast, capable of interacting with outside influences and are able to maintain our emotions and thoughts, thus our actions are consciously and consistently. More often, though, our systems are not as capable of competing with the conflicting aspects of outside information or situations and can be influenced to veer off the course of our normal mode of operation and into ineffective and less-than-ideal actions. This could be a moment when we experience high stress and anxiety or anger, leading us to react rashly and make less intentional decisions. These moments, where we are agitated or not confident in our orientation, lead us to want to get to the end of this situation at the cost of our future selves.

This is what most investors think when they see a sudden dip in the market. They see the value of their portfolio dropping and may not fully grasp why. They scramble to make sense of it and make a plan, they take their eyes off the long-term goal, and move to sell their positions to avoid more loss. Statistically, the market as a whole will bounce back, leveling out and going up with time, but the pain of seeing your investments in the red is excruciating at the moment. How you react in these situations helps you reveal something very important. It influences how you make big decisions, how you invest, and how you react. It is your personal risk tolerance.

Risk tolerances are how much risk you are comfortable taking and how you weigh losses against gains. Do you like skydiving, or is the thrill not worth the danger? Are you comfortable gambling, or do you hate the uncertainty and chance of loss? Large amounts of wealth are generally made in two ways: by slow diligence or high risk. Time really is money here. If you want a million dollars in your investment account and can save a thousand dollars a month, it would take you eighty-three years to hit your mark. If you deposit that into the market and get a modest seven to nine percent average annual return, you should have a million dollars in your account in 27 years. Or, after about two and a half years, you could also place $29,000 on lucky number 7 on a roulette wheel and beat the one-in-thirty-five odds. The chances of you losing that money is pretty high, but you could hit your goal. If the thought of placing that much money in a bet makes you a little squeamish, you probably have a reasonable to low risk tolerance. If you are currently trying to finagle ways to try and save a little more or better bets to place to see how you could make the casino route work to your advantage, then you probably have a higher tolerance for risk.

    Risk is also directly correlated with your knowledge and understanding. If you have little to no knowledge of the risk you are taking, it naturally will increase the risk. You didn't read the rule book, so you aren't fully informed. Likewise, if you are familiar with the area you are investing in, it isn't quite as scary. I still would not endorse roulette as a wealth-building strategy, but there are much better ways to play roulette than putting all your money on one number one time, which would increase your likelihood of any return at all. Risk is inevitable. Life is so dangerous; none of us make it out alive. One way to reduce your risk of loss is simply through knowledge and understanding of the rules and likelihoods. All investing requires risk. Markets will crash, and something will certainly cause you setbacks at some point, even if you choose the most conservative route. The other thing that reduces risk is contingencies. Even if you are taking risks, you should have a plan for what you will do if things go wrong. Do you have a backup plan? What is the worst that could happen, the likelihood of it, and what would you do? Regardless of what you find, your risk tolerance is to take calculated risks, because your tolerance will fluctuate.

    As you move through life, there is a moment when you realize that you may have more life behind you than in front of you. Sometimes you are confronted with the reality that you have more to lose than money. Your responsibility to partners and family will guide you to some conservatism. Becoming a parent is particularly humbling. Knowing that there are people whose well-being is directly influenced by your decisions will really make you think twice about the consequences attached to risk. You will find yourself more reluctant to take that career risk or take on riskier hobbies. You have something to lose. I encourage you to have the courage to take some calculated risks. Risk-taking is like a muscle that needs to be worked out. Too much can hurt you, but regular risk-taking opens up new levels of creativity and offers you a chance to prove that you can push through to achieve more with calculation and effort.

Assessing your abilities is a bit more straightforward. Put simply, what can you do? What are you good at? I must differentiate that this is not an interest; while interest makes it easier to hone and advance your abilities, it isn't always important. Today, you can learn many skills, but some things do come naturally to some extent. Motor skills are a great example.

Motor skills are the voluntary actions that involve our muscles. It's what helps us move. Athleticism is developed, but I am sure that we all know someone, or are that someone, for whom balance and graceful movement come more difficult. Some of this can be improved through training and exercise, but some of it comes naturally. Same with things like attention, learning styles, and creativity. There are those for whom these things come more easily just from the way that they are wired.

My six-year-old daughter understands this perfectly. She knows that one of her special powers is that she can write with both hands. She sees that many others can't. That is all that it takes. What are your special powers that differentiate you from a large percentage of your peers? Less impressive sounding though, what

Take Your Assessments

are you slightly better at than most, or what are you less good at than the average person? There is no shame in not being good at something or even being average. Your special talents may not even be that useful in most scenarios. It isn't what these things are that makes them important to catalog and assess; it is how you use them and account for them as you go about life.

One of the most controversial abilities to account for is intelligence. This isn't to limit anyone's capabilities to their IQ scores. IQ stands for Intelligence Quotient. It is a test and a score that measures things like pattern recognition, processing speed, verbal reasoning, and spatial awareness. These items are assessed, and they give you a score based on it. The US military popularized these scores during WWI, when they administered about two million of these tests and began using the data to determine what jobs individuals would be best suited for. A lot of the world followed suit to some degree and applied this to work and other parts of society. The average IQ worldwide is calibrated to be one hundred, with only about four percent having thirty-point variations.[10] So only two percent of the population is over one hundred thirty, and two percent less than seventy.

IQ tests and scoring are far from perfect; it is a test, and test-taking in itself is a skill, but worse, it also paints a very generalized picture of a limited number of factors. Furthermore, while it can help assess how you may do at certain careers, it isn't a direct correlation either way. In many cases, I would, in fact, discourage you from learning your scores. Few jobs require IQ tests, and for most intents and purposes, it is a vanity metric.

Your Emotional Quotient, or EQ, is arguably more important

in gauging your abilities. EQ measures your ability to understand, use, and manage your emotions in a positive way. This helps you manage stress, read and react to others, and keep things like depression and anxiety at bay. Some of the highest-paying jobs in white collar sectors today rely more on EQ than IQ to be successful. From the CEO who can keep their composure in high-stress times to the Salesperson who can read and match their client's moods and energy, EQ helps you not make the critical errors that our emotions tend us towards through stress, anger, and negativity.

There is a field of study within biology called epigenetics that is doing a lot of good work around nature and nurture, as well as how much of ourselves is actually in our control. So, in talking about IQ and EQ, it is really easy to beat yourself up for not being smarter or more in control of your emotions. Epigenetics gives us a pass to participate in one of our favorite pastimes here, blaming our parents. Depending on the study and variables, it is said that sixty to eighty percent of our IQ is based on genetics. So, if we take that as gospel, most of the IQ that you have will be more or less inherent, and you will likely end up around the level of your parents. EQ, on the other hand, is nearly flipped. EQ is found to be between ten to forty percent inherited, leaving up to ninety percent of your EQ as something that can be nurtured or developed.

I say all this, again, not to box anyone into a sense of determinism, but rather to expose IQ as more of a natural ability and not tied directly to your efforts or necessary in personal success. I am pushing back on the narrative of IQ being a critical success indicator in the hopes that, rather than relying on some test to tell you where your intelligence stacks up against the greater population, simply understand the level of normal and extraordinary, and allow yourself to assess not only your intelligence, but those you interact with. Then, following that, apply your honed EQ to interact with grace and understanding. Naturally, just when you feel like you have this figured out and you are feeling like you are smart, you can assess yourself against the Dunning-Kruger effect.

The Dunning-Kruger[11] effect is the humbling concept that is often parroted when describing clickbait topics like "why stupid people think they are smart." The concept centers around the journey of developing expertise through a graph that measures confidence and competence. It will start with Unconscious incompetence, which is what generates so many articles. This is where you very genuinely feel like you know more than you do, because you don't know what you don't know. It is easy to look at most things on the surface, ignore the complications, and feel like you know enough about the subject to operate as if you are informed. Then, as you move through your journey of knowledge acquisition, you realize your lack of knowledge and enter the phase of Conscious Incompetence, where you finally learn that there are things you don't know and begin proactively seeking the knowledge needed to close your newfound gap in understanding. During this search, with any luck, you will find yourself drifting to Unconscious Competence. This is where you are now, in a state of flow. You know enough that you no longer think of your knowledge of the subject as new, but normal. You know how and why you know what you know, and this is often when you find out if you are good at passing on your knowledge. Passing on knowledge is a talent, and it may not be yours, but trying to bring people up to speed on your knowledge has many perks. You not only reduce some of your headaches of being a passenger on someone else's journey through the Dunning-Kruger graph, but you are also participating in solidifying your understanding. Teaching helps you see new angles of a concept, outline new potential challenges, and humbles you to the difficulty of acquiring new knowledge. Few things will make you feel better than watching someone struggle to grasp a concept and being able to help them through it. Einstein summed this concept up when he said, "If you can't explain it simply, then you don't understand it well enough." Anything worth knowing is worth being able to share.

Your abilities can still only take you so far, though. Therefore, the last assessment should be your motivations. You can think of your motivations for why you do something, or you can think of your interest in doing something at all. You will find that you may have a talent for things and no real interest in them. Interests and motivations fade. Think of the musical prodigy who spent so much time with their instrument that they became bored and unchallenged, with no desire to pursue the title of "best." Understanding and abilities will grow and compound over time in many cases, like it or not. Motivations will ebb and flow. When aligned with other aspects, your motivations will give fuel to any fire that is burning and increase your performance and rate of taking in new information. Likewise, when it is low, it can starve all efforts and leave you with only small and labored gains, if any. Keeping an eye on your motivations should be frequent, monitoring for changes, and bolstering whenever possible to sustain the drive towards a long-term goal. It must be said, motivations are not goals. Motivations are not executable. Motivations are your overarching whys. Your goals are tied to outcomes, and you can put in effort to execute against them. It is easy to confuse your goals and motivations, after all, a goal can be very motivating, but if you can separate the two, then you can nurture them both to fuel optimization of your pursuit of a goal with all its executable actions and the purpose to continue the pursuit of it.

Momentum is a big part of life and success. As you grow older, you expand and grow your knowledge, making most things a little easier as you repeat the tasks. As you stay in a career field, your experience, competency, and pay will likely increase from training to when you retire or change fields. Likewise, as you maintain your investment plans, your portfolio will grow. Few things in life will hit you with a total loss, but a shift in direction can slow your momentum and cause setbacks. For instance, if you have a decade-long career as a plumber, then decide to make a leap to banking, you will probably see a huge barrier to entry and a pay cut due to your previous experience and lack thereof related to the task at hand.

Your motivations most certainly will change as you progress through phases and seasons in life. Your interests will change, your fears will change, and all this can greatly impact your short-term decision-making and even your long-term goals. Finding the largest anchors of motivation as early as possible that you can sustain as long as possible will be the most critical role in your journey and success. As mentioned earlier, though, fundamental misalignments cause so much damage to our progress and confidence. I encourage trying to identify the things that you fall back on as the things that mean the most to you from an early age, that you could follow through to death as your compass. Is it wealth, security, family, health, or a combination? This is because your motivations will be inextricably tied to your goals. Your natural self will find a way to gravitate towards what it believes are the highest goals. In a way, you subconsciously know what you should be doing and what is important. So often, our anxieties and recurring sense of being lost are because we deviate from our internal bearings and act as if they are wrong. When you feel discontent at a job, not because of the work or pay, but its restrictive or meaningless nature. When you stay in what you know to be a bad relationship, and muster up endless excuses to make it seem like the correct decision. Maybe it is as simple as your conscience coming in when you know you are doing something wrong. Oftentimes, we replay these events long after they happened and develop a "trauma" around them, preventing us from moving on with our lives. It's the pain of an almost physical split of our natural guidance system and our actions going in separate directions and creating a duplicate and less ingenious version of ourselves. Listen to your conscience; it will allow you and enable you to do much more than you likely give it credit for. Your conscience wants you to succeed and be happy, but it wants you to achieve those things in a healthy way.

You will, without a doubt, find times and instances where your short-term and long-term motivations are at odds. Do you take that little trip that you wanted for relaxation and experience, or do you put that money into your investment account? Do you work on your side project or sit on the couch and decompress with a little TV? These are your tactical and strategic motivations, and they shouldn't be seen as a dichotomy in conflict. Your tactical motivation operates on a shorter-term basis. Hunger is very much a tactical motivation. If you are working on something and get hungry, you can pause and eat, then get back to your work. You can really enjoy the meal and take pleasure in what you are eating. Likewise, you can eat something that you enjoy less and still achieve a full stomach.

Choose your experience. The maybe unseen or unnoticed part is the lack of productivity or quality of work that you may start to suffer if you power through working while you are hungry. Any parent or partner can tell you that a few things bring out the worst in people, like when they are hungry. There is a phenomenon dubbed "the hungry judge effect" that describes how US judges tend to be less lenient in sentencing and granting parole based on the time since their last meal. These are people that we look to for interpretation and enforcement of the law and its intentions. They can hold someone's future in their hands. Moreover, to become a judge requires experience and elections, and vetting to ensure a high degree of integrity, fairness, and intent in their rulings. The idea that these people in these situations and at scale could fall prey to something as mundane as the concept of hangry should tell us how susceptible we all are to simple negative stimuli.

    Yielding to tactical motivations is actually a great thing. While our short-term needs and wants may logically act in complete defiance of our long-term goals, they are important. They help us maintain contentment in the longer journey. They can keep us invigorated to stay the course while maintaining some level of sanity. There are many pleasures in life that we forgo for the betterment of our future selves, but if we are only concerned with the future version of ourselves and not our current selves, we may not like who we become. Missing out on small joys and memories for incremental gains later can hurt if you are not weighing the benefits against the cost in a way that is friendly, loving, and forgiving to yourself. Missing out on experiences will dull all the experiences in a full life. So leave some room for the short-term pleasures. Budget them in. There is a concept in personal finance called guilt-free spending, and it should be a budget line item. It is the padding in your monthly budget to allow for buying that outfit, ordering the appetizer and dessert, or going to that concert. These things will likely have little return that you could put a dollar value on, maybe even the contrary, and they seem like a waste, but they serve as the reward for what you are doing. Depending on the financial guru you are polling, guilt-free spending is normally going to be given a budget of ten to thirty-five percent of your wages. In the beginning phases of establishing your budget, it should be higher. Not because it is the most logical money move, but to start building habits without forcing deprivation that would discourage you from continuing on, due to the discomfort. If you can remain intentional and content, as you see movement towards your goal for a sustained length of time and the benefits it is starting to yield, you will find that the guilt-free spending budget will reduce, and the funds will slowly increase towards your goals. The habits are formed, the benefits revealed, and conscious and comfortable decisions can now be made.

Your strategic motivations should remain unwavering and a bit abstract, tied to a long-term goal. These are not targets so much as they are a general direction. It may be as simple as wanting to retire while you are young and healthy enough to enjoy it. So, at what age? It depends. So, with how much money? It depends. So does that mean that you will never work a job again? It depends. You cannot tell when and how your health will decline to where you would not consider yourself fit to enjoy your retirement, just like you cannot make the sweeping lifestyle decisions for a version of yourself half your lifespan in the future. You also don't get to choose how the economy reacts, whether it's the value of the currency or just the cost of bread. If you have a motivation towards a goal, you work as hard as you can at it, and the other items become clearer as you work your way through the journey. You must differentiate the motivations from the goals and outcomes. Motivating as the image of the goal of retiring on a beach at the age of fifty may be, the motivation to retire may simply be not to have to participate in the rat race you are running in until you die. The beach is just a nice consolation if you can make it work. One thing is certain, though. If you aim at a very small target, in a distant and unforeseen future, you are likely to miss it. Worse, you may hit it and realize that it wasn't what you wanted, or the work you put into it wasn't worth it after all. Minding your motivations and why you hold them helps unravel some of the confusion that we all hit at some point, where we are tied too much to the 'how' of our ideal lives playing out rather than the 'why' we are pursuing it at all.

True happiness is rarely tied to a goal. Happiness is more found in the flexibility you have to experience life while predicting the future just enough to feel secure and confident in it. When looking at these strategic and long-term goals, I am more in favor of them avoiding potential negative outcomes. Personally, I set one of my strategic motivations to simply never be poor again, and for my family not to worry about food or home insecurity. That is not seeking to be rich, but stable. I can adjust where and how I live, but that stability requires work, maintenance, and attention. It is not always easy, but I allow myself to have levers to pull to allow for more fun or less comfort and still keep on track with my motivation. That is a motivator that does not have an end. It will likely transfer to ensuring security for my grandchildren, and with any luck, great-grandchildren. It works in how I treat my kids and my partner because the stability I want is more than financial. It means I have to be content with my work to be able to continue to provide and have some capacity for them after the workday is done. It allows others to help me towards my goal, too, by building a community around a stable family. All the checks and balances are there for the long game, and that is what this life is: a long game.

So when assessing yourself, be honest, be kind to your past and future selves, and do not strive to be something you are not. I challenge you to consider these things and believe them. You are not your experiences to date, you are not your habits, you are not what others see in you, and you are not the outcome of your efforts. You transcend all those things, and you are exactly who you are supposed to be. Your outcomes are heavily influenced by your actions, decisions, sacrifices, and honed abilities, but are also subject to a great deal of luck. You are not assessing yourself against anyone else. This world is big and can support your uniqueness. At the same time, it has somewhat predictable rules. There are many things to learn about how things work, what things are more likely to produce positive outcomes, and what is more likely to produce negative outcomes. Take time to understand the arena that you find yourself in so you can apply your uniqueness in the fullest way, and allow you to impact more of your fellow humans directly. Your presence, gifts, and work may never impact the world in any way that you could put on a resume. But your world, your small corner of this wide world, and the people that share it with you can be beautiful and better because you are in it. The ability to shine bright, be comfortable in your skin, be happy, and apply yourself and your talents to better those around you will hinge on your ability to assess yourself. It will allow you the ability to make incremental and intentional improvements so that you can bring more of yourself to the table and experience the better parts of life in a real and compounding way.

SET YOUR GOALS

Goals are the ends to which we bend our means. Not everyone has them, long-term ones at least. They may have dreams, aspirations, or plans, but those are not goals. They may conflate them and even convince themselves that they have big life goals, but are they really? Dreams are things that you wait to happen, you wish to happen. It takes no action to have a dream, and there are no boundaries to how big you can dream. Aspirations are simply wishing for the best or highest achieving outcomes outside of all the things that push us to more average outcomes. Things that you work for and idealize. You take the achievement for granted because of the focus on an implanted dream. It does require effort and movement towards a goal, but with only the silver linings in view. Normally, aspirations will not look for where it can go wrong and fall short of the ideal, settling back to the average.

Aspirations leave us a way out and room to step away from the efforts without seeing it as failure. After all, we were aiming towards the best outcome, and it just didn't work out. Goals are the outcomes we make plans and work to achieve. It is a focal point, a target that you can hit with proper aim, practice, and dedication, and achieving your goal is mostly in your control and somewhat insulated from luck. Humans, more now than ever, should have such long-term goals. We need a destination for an outcome that takes decades to achieve. Some mission that can be tied to the life that you want to lead, it must be attainable and allow you to track your progress along the way. People who have true long-term goals, you will find, are fewer than one would think. You can have more than one, but for your goals, they should be tied to your ideal situations.

Long-term goals, especially, should be more about an idea rather than specifics in order to capture the essence of the intent. Retiring is a prime example of this. The goal is to have enough money to stop your career as you age and get a well-deserved, slower pace of life in your later years. Time to focus, reflect, and even repair some of the damage that was done in pursuit of money. This is going to be different for everyone, and you will have an idea of what that phase of life looks like for you. It takes planning for this. There are checkpoints and tactical actions that take place. There will be small changes along the way that will leave you with more or less resources to draw from by the time you decide it is time to cash in, but the goals are still intact. Tying retirement to a dollar amount set in your twenties or thirties will surely lead to unrealistic expectations. No one can predict the future, least of all economists. So with the best planning and information, you will not be able to say with any level of confidence the market, the value of your dollars, government support programs, or any real idea of what you truly need to survive and thrive in the sunset years. So what do you do? Well, what we all do. The best we can. We plan a squirrel away savings. We try to make smart investments to facilitate growth. We check in every so often on if what we are doing is working and we go about our lives with our goal in the back of our mind, because as long as we see acceptable movement in the direction of our goal and our plans are adequate and progressing on schedule, no further action is needed. The constant striving is necessary to keep up, but with any sense, it is routine and low maintenance.

Being on autopilot gives us room to make tactical or short-term goals and execute towards them with small, easy next steps. Short-term goals that are hopefully, at least, related to our long-term goals, but don't have to be closely linked. These can be a career goal that needs extra effort to achieve. It may be getting yourself out of the debt that you found yourself in. It could be finding your partner. All should be pursued with intention and require more resources than your set-and-forget long-term goals. These can roll up, unspecifically, to a long-term goal of where we want to be in life, but are focused on our shorter-term situation.

Tactical goals do not have to necessarily be tied to your long-term efforts, though. Building a framework of goal-setting in your life will give you a playbook to a way of thinking that delivers results. Making a large, consumer purchase is not something that ever proves useful in the world of saving for retirement, but in America, particularly, we attach a lot of value to these purchases and our image. That expensive wardrobe, the nice car, or an extravagant dining out habit; it would be hypocritical of most anyone in the modern, western world to condemn others for such purchases. There is nothing wrong with wanting or having nice things, but obtaining them without respect to the bigger picture can present issues. Sometimes that wardrobe or car is tied to the career you want. We would be foolish to think that our image does not play a role in how we are perceived in certain settings. That dining out habit could be your chance to network and progress socially, or even just stay connected to the community. The purchases, if budgeted and intentionally made, are not a problem. Problems only arise when these are big decisions and consumption of your precious resources is spent frivolously and without thought of their relation to our long-term goals. While they may not be directly related to our progress, they certainly can act against our progress toward long-term goals. Setbacks, small and large, towards our goals should be carefully examined, because just like our gains can compound and grow, so can our losses. A planned, one-time setback can be accounted for and budgeted in, but a habit that forms as a result is harder to work into long-term plans.

In the world of personal finance, there is the concept of "paying yourself first." This applies to a theory that you should pay into your savings and investing accounts before even your bills and other expenses. This helps fight the urge to see these investment funds as optional and something that you could possibly tinker with. This plays into your long-term goals. You know what you need to save each month to hit your savings goal in the allotted period, so stay on track. This goes hand in hand with conventional advice that this amount is ten to twenty percent of your earnings. I have always thought of it as a tax on my future self. A set amount, dictated by an authoritative body. Like taxes, if evaded, there will be consequences.

Ramit Seth[12] coined a concept around your budgets called the "Guilt-Free Spending" budget that says you should allot a set amount of your money towards guilt-free spending. Ten to twenty percent. This isn't the logical part of your budget. This is its own safety net against your irrational mind. Without this part of your budget, your frivolous purchases are subject to shame. They are seen as contradictory to your long-term goals. This aptly named guilt-free spending budget allows you to be human and have fun without feeling oppressed by your own budget. Since it is a percentage, its value increases with your earnings, so the better you do financially, the more spending your budget, allows for. The concept of guilt-free spending and having planned, but not productive items in your budget is more than money. It is your time as well. As you progress in life, picking up momentum and responsibility, time starts to reveal itself as your most precious asset. One that you do not realize is depleting until there is none left. You must be kind to your present self. Without that, you risk resenting your future self and growing into that role.

You should set all your goals to be realistically attainable. Not hitting goals can be devastating. Even if no damage is done in practice, your confidence can be deeply shaken. You set the goal, you planned it out, you poured your effort into it, and it wasn't enough to achieve what you set out to do. Why?! It could be from poor planning, you could have tried harder, Something unexpected swooped in and changed the landscape, or the world could have just gotten in the way. Every missed goal comes with its own set of reasons and excuses. Honestly, they are coping mechanisms aimed at displacing the disappointment you feel for the lackluster results. Which brings us to the last type of goal to have, and that is a stretch goal.

Stretch goals are commonly used in sales organizations and

are goals so high that no one expects you to hit, but the closer you get, the more incentivized you are. Goals are designed to be hit, like quotas. They should be attainable and missed only for preventable circumstances. Stretch goals provide a point of striving that helps you identify the best possible scenario, name it, and set incentives if you achieve higher than expected results. In the world of retirement planning, this is the difference between meeting the goal of retiring somewhat comfortably with an average pension comparable to your average salary and retiring on a beach in your lavish mansion. It's aiming for an average career that pays well enough, but is turning out to be a CEO. Your long-term stretch goals are your ideal life, only achievable if you exceed your goals wildly at every step of the way and fall into some insane luck, too.

    An exercise to identify what your stretch goals are in life is to start by imagining that money is not an issue. Don't imagine that you won the lottery and have unlimited money to buy all the greatest things life has to offer. Just imagine that you have your dream job that leaves you happy, engaged, and feels purposeful while doing it. Imagine that it just happens to pay enough money to give you all you need to be completely content. What does that life look like? "Fuck you money" is a modern buzzword that helps conceptualize this, too. That is summed up as the amount of money that you have in your account that would allow you to tell the entire world that you don't need them and their money, so you are going to do what you want. What is that dollar amount, and if you had it, what would you be doing next? This gives you two stretch goals right away. What is your dream life, and how much money do you really need to achieve that level of independence? Let's not kid ourselves, these are not things that the majority of people will achieve. The odds of winning the lottery are close to one in three hundred million, not worth counting on. But knowing what these things are gives you a tangible point to execute against. To assess your deeper desires when it comes to a happy life so when you see opportunities to move closer to the ideal, you can seize them with intention.

When you are looking at all these goals, though, you really have to start considering your needs and wants. In the English language, we use this interchangeably every day. We don't just need food, we need sushi. We don't just need a friend, we need a ride or die companion. We don't just need a place to live, we need a five-bedroom house in the hip part of town, immaculately decorated to feel at home. Our needs blur with the ideals, and we find it insulting and beneath us to consider settling for less. Now we all have slightly different needs to thrive, but elevating your needs to excess misaligns all the targets to hit. We need so much less than we give ourselves credit for. We can survive and have a great life without many of the luxuries that we are sold on a daily basis from the various media sources we take in. Furthermore, there are billions of people in this world who have a very significantly lower standard of living than we have set as our baseline. Are you really that much more than they are that your needs should exceed theirs so much? Is your humanity more than theirs that you require more to simply exist on this earth? It is worth noting that many of the nations that have a third or less of the prosperity of America have longer lives, more happiness, and higher birth rates.

Just like interest compounds, so do our needs. We get a taste of comfort and get used to it. We get a taste of luxury, and we want more. So, the opposite side of visualizing goals, imagine what your base level of survival is. Imagine that your credit has been taken away, and you are in a cash-only society. What would you buy and how would you live, starting with nothing? Imagine your neighbors are in the same boat, so comparison is not an issue. How would your days look, and what would your goals be then? We live in a time and place of immense wealth and comfort, and the reality is that it is not truly necessary. Nice, but not necessary. The productivity that so many seek is often not true productivity, but busyness, which helps us feel as if we earn our keep, but leads to stress, burnout, and nihilism. Our wants and mischaracterized needs coax us into a place where we become the center of our world and make it easier to lose sight of the real reasons we even work in the first place.

    Living below your means is at the top of the list for every expert who aims to lead their audience to any sort of financial freedom. Simply because it is a lot easier to manage your money and save if you are not spending everything you have. The easiest way to do this is to align your goals with true needs. Set your dream lifestyle low enough that you do not have to constantly labor over keeping it. Make it attainable with less than average outcomes. Lastly, in times of wild success, rather than increasing the goals of comfort, decrease the time to reach them. When thinking of your retirement or any other financial goal. If you have an extra thirty thousand dollars and you can add it to your retirement goal. You can adjust your plan to account for a hundred dollars more a month or stick to your plan and start retirement three years earlier. Assuming ten thousand dollars a year is your normal savings rate, using the four percent rule. This is a simple example, and many times it may make sense to build a little more of a stockpile if you do not have enough built into your plans. Maybe you are happy and content, but your days are numbered and are not getting any younger. Time is only worth so much money.

With our culture being so focused on comparisons to each other and our mental models being created by external cues of success, it is worth a venture into defining what the average citizen can expect. In 2024, it is reported that the median income in the US is about ninety-eight thousand dollars, and the average household income is sixty-eight thousand dollars. According to a world population review, American households spend an average of sixty-one thousand dollars a year. With all the talk of the housing market increasing, the median home cost is about two hundred seventy thousand dollars, and the median rent is around eleven hundred dollars. The average home size is around two thousand four hundred square feet.

Consider this in contrast to the UK, a notable first-world country. The average income there is roughly thirty-eight thousand pounds, and the median is around thirty-two thousand pounds. The average home price is around two hundred eighty thousand pounds, and the average home size is a little more than eight hundred square feet. A seemingly large difference in living expectations for two of the larger Western cultural bastions.

There are big differences between average and median, as would be expected with more lower-paying jobs than higher-paying, but the average is probably less telling than you would imagine. For example, if you packed Wembley Stadium with people of zero net worth and had Warren Buffett deliver a talk, the average net worth of all in attendance would be over a million dollars.[13] Not very helpful. Median is in some ways more useful for goal-setting benchmarks when it comes to gauging yourself against a large population to ensure you are considering aspects like full-time employment, as well as high and low income earners. So, as great as these numbers are, they are going to present some true comparison issues. You have to hold those benchmarks far enough out to really see what they mean. Try to ignore the outliers; the insanely wealthy. Strip away the signals of wealth that could be purchased on a credit card and look to true signifiers of personal wealth. Do you have control of your own life and your time? Are you truly adding value to others around you, and do they know it? How fragile is your system, and what are the things that could cause your life to crumble? The shift of seeing success in your own self versus others' lives will drastically affect the way you think of what success is. Too often, we see people wrapped in material success and think, "Wouldn't it be nice to live that life. They have it all." When in reality, we are only seeing the image they put forward. We don't see what they sacrificed to signal that success. Wild success often comes with work that crushes other key aspects of life. It comes with sacrificing relationships. It can also come with stress, habits, and problems that people without that level of extravagance do not have to deal with. Therefore, we should never envy what someone else has, because you don't know what it took to get it.

While many of the numbers have changed quite drastically from the days when I found myself planning my goals out for the first time, much of it remains true, still. When I found myself trying in college and starting to plot out one of the biggest decisions in life of what I should do as a career, I heard a clip of The Dave Ramsey Show where they discussed the annual salary that produces the most happiness. This segment threw out that the optimal salary for happiness was seventy-five thousand dollars per year. While, come to find out later, there was research done by Daniel Kahnman from Princeton University that hypothesizes that "High income improves evaluation of life but not emotional well-being," so it wasn't unfounded, this number.[14] I never read the research, but took it away and thought about why I thought it sounded legitimate. I marinated on that and its possible, pithy reasons as to why. Here is why I believed that seventy-five thousand dollars per year was so magical.

First, it is attainable. This is above the average wage, yes, but that is the beauty of it. The average wage numbers include a high number of lower-wage, non-career jobs, part-time work, and early career positions. All of which would be expected to be below someone's earning potential. Is it attainable by salary and a flat, forty-hour work week? Maybe not, but with overtime and dedication to a career, it is. I had the privilege in my career to work with many great people with little to no education who could clear the six-figure mark. Did they work harder than I did? Definitely. Did I want their job, not necessarily. They knew that this was their shot to make good money, though, and they did.

Secondly, it requires some degree of expertise. You likely are going to need a job that you are good at, have some experience in, and that not everyone can do. This provides a lot of satisfaction and pride in your career. It helps you see the value in your work and gives you a bit of a sense of pride and purpose in your work. This is why the pay is above average, because you are above average in this field. The added benefit of this level of experience is that it can allow for a sense of predictability in your responsibilities. This range will often be for individual contributors or lower-tier managers, allowing for a more standard work week. Once you have developed your niche, you will have some level of job security and career opportunities to negotiate and maintain something of a balance.

Third, it can meet basic needs. In the majority of the US and the world, seventy-five thousand dollars, despite buzz topics of the impossible cost of living, can provide a stable lifestyle. After twenty percent in taxes, you are left with five thousand dollars per month in spending. This fits in the model for your rent or mortgage at the twenty-five percent mark and, with a frugal lifestyle, can provide food, transportation, and entertainment. A five percent emergency fund saving rate can keep you out of too much trouble, and at a seven percent retirement savings rate, you will have around one million dollars after a forty-year career, all things remaining stagnant. Is it a lavish life, not necessarily, but it can be a life of enough. If you plan on introducing a partner into the picture, any supplemental income allows for notable comfort increases as well as savings potential.

Finally, in perspective, this income level will put you in the top twentieth percentile of the world in wages and quality of life. Steering away from the terminology of middle-class, this puts you in the range of the everyman. You will be able to interact with a little of the lower class and a little of the upper class, how they live, and get a better view of the landscape. The benefit of this is perspective. You can see a path to more achievement and possibly the stress it would take to get there, but you can also see a less affluent side of life that you wish to avoid for yourself. It isn't pity or prowess, but a way of staying in touch with our world and our fellow man. In the middle, compassion is more easily found. Acceptance is more easily achieved, and the opportunity for small but meaningful change is abundant.

Slightly above average in an attainable way is a noble goal to hold economically. Again, the average is the life that the majority of your peers and fellow humans will fall into. On my journey, I opted only for just a little more. The one-hundred-thousand-dollar mark was a benchmark I had set for myself. At that time, I did not know anyone who made that much money, so to me, that was rich. I also set my fuck you money goal as one million dollars, because at the time, I knew that I could ride that out for a majority of my life since I did not need much to live at the age of eighteen. Now the fuck you money was updated as I grew in my career, as I became a little more savvy and realized it would be fine to retire at the age of sixty or after, but if I hit that number by forty, it probably was not going to quite support a family, and I should work a little longer. The goal of one hundred thousand dollars a year in pay, never adjusted. It took a while to get there. My first job out of college paid forty thousand dollars and demanded fifty-hour weeks. I was able to secure new positions and build a career in an industry. The first time I hit my salary goal, I was thirty-two, married, and with two kids. I had come close with side hustles a few years ago, but I had made it. I even exceeded it at times in my thirties by a notable amount. It took a decade of very hard work, long hours, mistakes, learnings, and sacrifices, but I made it. I did not have a degree that guaranteed high earnings, I did not choose an easy industry, but for my seniority, I was paid above average. Yes, I made it.

I found a few things out about the one-hundred-thousand-dollar salary goal in my experience. First, it takes commitment. Aside from the years of experience that I had to accumulate, it gets harder to change positions at that pay rate. At the six-figure level, companies want more loyalty and time in all the companies on your resume. Less than eighty thousand per year, I found that I could get jobs significantly faster, as well as train in a shorter amount of time. Above that, it took much more effort to move organizations. Next, there was the responsibility. I found that in the type of work that I did, and from others I knew and could speak to in confidence, it seemed like every dollar above about ninety-five thousand per year added more expectation, stress, time, and frustration. Especially in smaller companies, middle and upper management got to see all the stress of the executive suite; as an individual contributor, you had to be extra valuable because you knew that your name would be reviewed first in staff reductions. Lastly, at that earning level, finding the next rung on the ladder got harder. By that time, I had held many different positions and responsibilities and started to see much more that I did not want to do than things I did. Chasing this slightly higher salary tied a lot of my identity to my work and my compensation. That is not uncommon. The pursuit of success becomes a part of the job and adds to the work and mental load you are under. I saw a few higher-paid coworkers who felt they could get out of office social events, working late, and putting up with toxic behaviors because they knew they couldn't stop playing the game. The ones that did opt out of those things did not last long for one reason or another. Yes, I came to find that the most toxic work cultures start to infiltrate most at a specific pay range.

      Mostly, I found that most of the money past my goal did not really add much more to my personal career satisfaction. The confidence boost that I got from the prestige came with more stress that, in a short while, crushed my mental health and led me to spend more money to try and alleviate my stress. I found myself simply trying to maintain my target salary and get more perks, easier work, less stress, and most importantly, some of my time back. I had decent stuff, a modest house in a neighborhood I liked, decent used cars with less than a hundred thousand miles on them, food on the table, and most importantly, time with my family that I wasn't as willing to give up.

It took a long time to fight the urge to be important at work, but I was constantly telling myself that these were the things that I was working for: a good life with my family. I saw a meme that ended up replaying constantly and at times was even a background on my work computer. It read: "No one at your job will remember all those times you worked late, but your children will." It is true, and when you blink and they get older, and it starts to set in, that time is the only resource you cannot replenish. Not just your time, but your kid's time, your parents' time, your time with your partner or your family. You cannot roll back the clock with those you love.

All this feeds into the idea that your goals are more than dollar amounts, titles, and achievement. It is more about the life you want to lead and the legacy you want to leave. I knew long before I met my partner, before the idea of having children started to sound good to me, and even before I made the choice to go to college and what I would study, that what I really wanted was a balanced life and a family legacy. I wanted what I never had growing up: a stable, healthy family. I wanted to give my children a good life, but not be corrupted by a silver spoon, so they would be resilient. I wanted to be able to pass my learnings down and to be loved in return. I wanted a marriage that was a real and lasting partnership like my grandparents had, but with less bickering brought on by economic stress. I wanted to be a role model of how things could work out if you just did the right things. I knew that work and money would play a critical role in this, so I plotted the balance I saw as achievable and allowed room for all this. Could I have made more money, yes, but I factored that in early on. I knew that there were sacrifices that would have to be made and risks that I would have to take. I knew that getting more meant a chance of failure, and I did not factor failure into my goals, only contingencies if bad luck struck. The stretch goals and optimism remained in place; there is always room to take a step back. There is always room to do more when needed, but I hold tight still to your goals being an optimization of your efforts and not a maximization of your outcomes.

No matter your plans, you can always do more, but setting your minimum requirements gives you the point that you can reach them, take a breath, and accept that you have and are doing enough. Knowing when enough is enough is a talent, an art, and a hard realization to embody. Normally, when someone says "enough is enough," they are at wits' end and ready to quit, but it bends the words to only use it only in a negative connotation. In fact, "enough is enough" is the ultimate phase of contentment. I have enough, and that is enough for me. I don't need any more, so I will not pursue it. If nothing more comes, I am ok with that.

Do you know where your "enough" line is before you get close to it? Do you know where something is no longer worth the time, effort, and resources for the benefit you get, and can you even accurately assess that benefit? In your work, how many new things, stress, and extra hours can your boss add before you say it is not worth it unless concessions are made with more pay or more help? Do they know that line? We hear all the time about people feeling like they are being mistreated, underappreciated, or even abused, but does the other person really know? In relationships of any kind, we all have bad periods where we are selfish and aloof. Normally, it is due to situations and stressors we may not even realize that cause us to need and even demand more of those around us, and it is not always fair. If you are on the receiving end, though, it has to be called out, and it can be done unemotionally and kind. You would not express that your boundaries are being encroached on if you did not care to continue the relationship in a healthy way. In your relationships, in your job, and even in your hobbies, when you are pursuing anything that requires your investment, know what the stakes are and where things become not worth it anymore. Telling the other party that you have a boundary and things are getting close to it should result in an acknowledgement that the line exists. You will get pushback. This is just gravity. There was forward motion towards your boundary, speed, and momentum. Expecting a hard stop is not realistic. You have to allow some room to come to a stop and back up. Allow this grace. If you went headfirst into a hobby and it crossed that boundary of invading your productive time and taking away from your progress towards your goals, the idea that you can just stop if it got that far is not likely. You will need to wean off a little. Same same for your boss, and all the other relationships you may have that will challenge your limits. It may be a good thing to move your boundaries to adjust for these relationships. It may be worth it, but do it with intention and assessment.

   You must align your sense of enough with your goals. More money for the same amount of time and stress at your job, great! Less money for a while for the career you want, fine. More friction or distance in your relationship to allow your partner to grow, acceptable. The question is, how do these align with your goals and why? If these things run the risk of leading you in a different direction, it may take some serious thought on if your goals are still the direction you want or need to be heading. Many things in life serve as a catalyst for change, and changing your goals is always an option. The key is changing them and not eliminating them. As we grow and change ourselves, our desires can as well. Our situations can be drastically altered and render our plans insufficient. New experiences can change our whys and leave them requiring fundamental updates. Children have a way of doing that. You may or may not want children for all sorts of reasons, but one thing is certain and that is once you have children, you will no longer think the same. It is proven that mothers and fathers alike go through significant physical and psychological changes once their offspring come into the picture. There are no books, lectures, or self-reflection that can help you determine how you will change, but you will. All of a sudden, your life has a sense of purpose and responsibility that exists outside yourself. New forms of emotion start to appear as never before. Joy, worry, fear, anxiety, pride, guilt, and optimism all have new degrees to them related to the independent human that you brought into existence. I always wanted to be a parent and was terrified of it, so I planned for it. I knew that I did not want to alter my goals around kids, so I built them into my plans from day one. I knew, though, that there would be life before them and life after them. About twenty years of child rearing, from expenses to time. After that, if all went according to plan, I would have fully functioning adult children and could prepare for retirement and grandparenting with more time and resources at my disposal.

Children are not the only thing that can change your plans, though. Some things can be much more unexpected and not have a nine-month prep time. Your health is a time bomb that few people factor in. Your entire livelihood is tied to your health, from your job to your sanity. When planning things out in your twenties and thirties. The average life expectancy in the world is about seventy-two years old; it varies by country and sex, with places like Hong Kong having an average of eighty-five, and many African countries having as low as fifty-two. This statistic can set you up with false hope on both sides. While most hope for a long life, if you are planning for this, your retirement plans should mirror this. Inflation increases over time, devaluing your savings, and will eventually get the best of even the four percent rule. Most people in their twenties today do not feel that they will have benefits like Social Security when they reach that age, for many good reasons. Therefore, the fear of running out of money in retirement if you live longer than average is not unfounded. More frightening, though, a short life is every bit as likely as a long one. If one in seven people in the US can expect to live to ninety, the law of averages says that one in seven also won't make it to fifty. If you look at graphs of mortality by age, the first notable tick up starts around fifty-five. Does your plan account for this? Sure, the money factor gets a bit easier, but if your health declines in your fifties, did you build enough living into your plans early on?

    I have mentioned it before, but I believe in breaking your life into phases. This concept is well laid out in the Hindu faith with the four life stages. Stage one is the student phase, where you lay a foundation of knowledge to prepare you for life. The second and most important is the householder phase, where you focus on virtue, producing, growing wealth, and building a family. Third is the forest dweller stage, where you focus on spirituality. Few people actually enter this stage and pass it by. Lastly, there is the wise stage, where you can begin to detach from life and prepare to die.

I have always broken it out in a more Western-based system. In your teens, try to find who you are. In your twenties, work hard and establish yourself while you have energy and flexibility. In your thirties, build mastery and focus on expertise. In your forties, plan your escape. In your fifties, start to coast through the work. In your sixties, transfer your knowledge. In your seventies, relax into your communities and routines that can sustain you to the end. Again, the twenties through forties are the most important. The work and investments you make as early as possible build momentum. You build expertise and habits, good and bad, that will dictate your level of execution and success, and the greatest of the habits are your own needs and wants. Picking up expensive tastes and poor work habits in your twenties is very hard to convince yourself away from in your forties. As habits go, the longer you hold them, the harder they are to break.

Minding your momentum is more difficult than we give it credit for. Normally, you will hear momentum being talked about in the sense of how easy things can be when you get momentum. It is not as sexy to talk about building that momentum from nothing. It is hard. That old Confucian line of "a journey of a thousand miles begins with a single step" doesn't express the difficulty of mile ten when you are tired, sore, and questioning why you are taking this journey anyway.

Your portfolio is like that. Charlie Munger famously said, "the first hundred thousand is a bitch, but you gotta do it." Boy, is it. That first hundred thousand, if you save around eight hundred and fifty dollars per month, will take you roughly eight years to hit with a seven percent average annual return. That eight hundred fifty dollars a month is a lot early on, too. You are likely at your lowest rate of income, and you aren't seeing the returns in any meaningful way. The next hundred thousand, though, at the same saving amount (not percentage), will only take five years. The next, less than four, and soon your interest will exceed your contributions. Forty years with no changes in contribution, and you could expect to have about two million investments. It takes that momentum, though; if you take a year off or reduce your contributions, it will likely cost you. If you take a riskier investment and have losses, it will cost you. Any disruption in that formula takes you farther away from your expected portfolio value.

That momentum towards your goals is something that must be maintained and sustained. That is why your goals have to be attainable and not just under ideal conditions, because things are rarely ideal. Furthermore, they have to be run for as long as possible, because while a pivot can keep you headed in a similar direction, it could cause disruptions in that linear flow, and that is painful from a progress standpoint as well as a personal standpoint - Habits and all.

So, if there is a theme that you could glean from most of this section on setting your goals, I hope that it is not guidance on what your goals are, why they are your goals, or even how to execute on those, but instead, just one thing: intentionality. Set your goals with intention. Thought out, realistic, sustainable intention. Everything you do, if done with intention that is set in realistic expectation, will allow you to maintain momentum toward where you want to be. Your intentions will help show you who you really are and what is actually important to you. Your intentions will grow in tandem with your conscience and help you execute your every task with conviction.

Set Your Goals

Know why you want what you want and do not want. Act in consideration of the end you have in mind, and work for your future self. Help that version of you have all they want and leave them with as few regrets as possible. That future version of yourself will thank you for it as long as you did it all with proper, planned intention.

STAKEHOLDERS AND SHAREHOLDERS

I remember a concept from my Business 101 class. Admittedly, it stuck with me, because at seventeen and in my first semester in college. I got the questions wrong on a test. I knew I shouldn't have, but did, and I never forgot it. Eventually, it became something that I sought to work into the way that I see my relationships. It was something to the tune of "What is the difference between a stakeholder and a shareholder?" These are terms that, if you work anywhere around finance or management, you hear often. I regularly hear people, who should know better, getting these terms mixed up. There are very important differences between the two, their relationships to a business, and how they should be considered in different situations. So let's clear this up and start with some definitions.

It is important when discussing shareholders that we understand shares. Shares are an individual unit of ownership in a company. A company, when raising capital for any reason, will issue parts of itself for sale, rather than asking for a loan. A loan will be for a set amount and to be paid back with interest and within a time period. A loan is principally a service to the company, where issuing shares brings in partners to share in the risk and rewards of the company's success. Issuing shares is often a less disruptive operationally and safer for the company financially because it removes the need to make payments and allows investment in strategy instead of transactions. When issuing shares, a company will obtain a valuation of its estimated worth based on its current financial situation and its potential for growth. Based on that valuation, the company then determines the number of shares it will issue and the price, effectively cutting itself into pieces to be sold. When issuing shares, the company must then become aware of who the shareholders are and the amount of the business they now own- their Stock. Stock is simply the percentage of a company you own based on your number of shares. Those who own a higher percentage of a company's shares and thus are more invested in the success of the company, then begin to have rights they can exercise, such as additional insight into the company's operation and projects, up to voting and consultative rights.

So, a shareholder is someone who holds shares of a company. A person who has a financial vested interest in the company. In many instances, shareholders of a certain size or investment get a vote on large company decisions. While these voting rights can vary widely depending on the structure of an organization, it is indicative of the mutual relationship between the business and the shareholder. Furthermore, shares hold a value, so they can be bought, sold.

A stakeholder is someone who simply has some sort of interest in something. I particularly like to think of it as someone with an interest in the company's success. In business, this is someone interested in the business and its operations or product, and can really encompass anyone who touches the business: managers, employees, customers, and shareholders.

Now, if you imagine yourself as a business. You probably can quickly identify the stakeholders in your life. Those who actively participate in your life and want the best for you. It is very easy to think of stakeholders as your acquaintances, classmates, coworkers, or even distant family that your mom loves to update on all the happenings in your life, but your list of stakeholders is much bigger than you may think. Your stakeholders are also those who your actions *could* affect. If you are driving, everyone on the road is one of your stakeholders. They, knowingly or not, want you to be ok and to be attentive so as not to cause an accident. If you have been driving for a while, you may think that it is a given that cars just happen to stay in their lane, but remember that the operator of that vehicle is a human just like you and easily capable of taking actions that could endanger everyone around them. You pick up and drop off stakeholders anytime someone is around. It's often overlooked how a polite word, a simple smile, grace in a frustrating situation, or inconsiderate selfish behavior can affect those around you. If you ever feel that your effect on the world is small and insignificant, really think about how many stakeholders you have encountered today and how valuable it is simply to do the best you can for them. Your effect on them may easily influence their network of stakeholders and can ripple out in good and bad ways. If you are the product that you offer to the world, from an advertising standpoint, you want all encounters to be positive and leave an impression. Not every marketing exposure generates a customer, but most customers are generated by marketing exposures. Put your best foot forward and be the light that you want to see reflected back.

Shareholders in your life, however, are those who have invested in you. They want to see their investment yield results. Like in business, not all shareholders are created equal. They are able to invest different amounts, and those who invest the most will have higher expectations of success or even could expect some participation in the process. Voting rights, if you will. There are three major types of shareholders that, with any luck, everyone will have at some point: Family, Teachers, and Friends. All three of these unique shareholder types are critical to development and striving. They will shift in their level of importance throughout life's phases, but never truly go away. Like in business, individual shareholders will come and go, but as they give up their shares, it frees you to take on more ownership or bring on new partners to fill the gap.

Some of the larger shareholders in your life will undoubtedly be your family. Families come in many shapes, sizes, and origins, but basically, these are the people who span all the phases of your life, from early to late, and are generally not chosen. They can include genetic parents, adopted families, extended families, and merged families. The origins are not as important as the intrinsic notion of responsibility to the family unit. There is a concept that blood is thicker than water, simply meaning that familiar relations deserve a level of loyalty to one's relatives that supersedes outside relationships and circumstances. While I do not think that sentiment is as widely held today, and I am not a full proponent of it absolutely, most would agree that a fringe member of your family, like the crazy uncle, gets more grace and tolerance within a family unit than a community at large. The beautiful thing about that is the understanding that you are afforded that same level of base support. Furthermore, the notion that the relationship is focused through a longer lens allows you to be yourself, grow, change, and remain supported, or at least accepted.

The most important aspect of the family, still, is the immediate. Most specifically, parents. They pour time and resources into your physical success and safety, they invest in your upbringing by trying the best they can to lay a foundation of how to operate in the world to the best of their ability, and they do this in most cases with limited claim to your future and any hopes of tangible return.

Now, even the best families are messy. There are no shortages of opinions, studies, and resources on how to parent children. However, there are not really many resources on how to be a child of a parent. One of the more modern narratives around "childhood trauma" is that children are blank slates and are solely impressions by their experiences. While that holds water in the idea that it is not a child's job to know better, and many times they are fully a victim of their parental circumstances, there is very little emphasis placed on that transition. It seems that as a child grows, they shift into their own consciousness overnight, and by the teenage years, they are seen as a developed person and shunted off into the world with a defeatist approach to further development. All of a sudden, parenting is expected to shift to a family colleague model, and nothing further can be done as the child is now an adult.

As in many phases throughout life, where you start to face transitions more consciously, there is an insane amount of reframing involved in the teenage years that can happen which helps shake off the trauma of the previous phase to move more towards the next. Striving for the highest possible level of closure should be taught as early as possible. As any child starts to move into adolescence, it serves one well to assess what it is like to be a parent and to have a bit of sympathy for the process. Understanding the investment that your own parents have made, despite the value you feel you received from them, helps to heal resentment and trauma. As a parent, telling the stories of your childhood and struggles with your parents helps. Let your kids know that your parents weren't perfect and highlight the differences. Tell them about the things your parents did that you, as a parent, would never do. Likewise, show them the other side. Tell them how you saw your parents struggle. How they got stressed to work and made time for extracurricular activities, how they dealt with the bills they weren't sure they could pay, or how you could tell that they hated their job, but did all that while raising you. It's not complaining, but it is dispelling the idea that anyone has these phases of life easily and that hardship in potentially infinite forms is inevitable, but the love and support are there. "Mother or father knows best" is not a claim of infinite wisdom, but instead it is a way of saying that your parents are your closest allies and want to apply their wisdom to your situation with your best interest at heart. They want to spare you the pain they went through. If they could do the hard things for you and take on your pain, they would. So, children, be receptive, kind, and forgiving when you look back at your parents. Understand that no one is perfect. Just as you are learning to walk through this world, they are too. There is no guidebook that actually works in parenting, and your individuality presents wonders and challenges no one could have foreseen. Know that with any luck, you will face the same one day. When that day comes, ask your parents how they did it and see how all the stress and struggle fade in hindsight, and all that is left is love and maybe some nostalgia.

While familial input is inevitably not always taken well, from ego, familiarity, or as Will Smith's song goes, "parents just don't understand," we seek and acquire more shareholders along the way. Your teachers, counselors, coaches, and others older and hopefully wiser than you, at least in some subject matter, are critical to development and progression. These people who place themself in positions to uplift others and invest in people on a large scale. Helping others is a love language that not everyone speaks. It takes a certain type of person to want to deal in this currency, and seeing the good they can bring out in others is the compensation they ultimately seek to get meaning and purpose. A teacher for example that was born in the 1990s would have gone through high school, then six to eight years of college, acquired thirty to one hundred thousand dollars of student debt all to come out of school to a fifty-five thousand dollar a year salary in possibly one of the most hostile education systems ever where they are expected to help students meet all the arbitrary test scores amid decreasing onus on children and parents in a social setting that no longer values the former bedrocks of learning such as literacy. No, it is not for the money or the cushy work conditions that anyone would agree to this type of torture; it is for the chance to invest in a large pool of developing humans in hopes that something takes hold and they can impact that individual or society as a whole in a positive way. One comment by a former student who remembers their efforts is enough to fill the tank for the next school year. These people are the ones who work tirelessly and thanklessly to be the light that they want to see in the world. These types of people are the ones that you should seek to find throughout your life. Their experience is deep, and they will expand it to meet your thirst for knowledge. They will help assess your capabilities and challenge you to do your very best while holding you accountable. They will connect you with the resources to achieve your goals as you progress and open many doors, and your receptiveness to their work helps perpetuate their gifts to others. I assure you that for every one person that truly learns from a good teacher, there are 50 that will not accept the gifts that they offer, and as that number grows, the light flickers. It will be a dark world once we turn our backs on these people who want to realize the best in us.

Finally, there are your friends. Friends and acquaintances, by nature, are the more volatile group of stakeholders and shareholders alike. Friends will generally be represented by those shared interests or proximity. They are made through frequent and meaningful interactions. They are normally relatively close in age or life phase and share similar values. As much as we can derive value from friendships with people vastly different from us in beliefs and walks of life, it isn't the norm. I would venture to say that having one to ten true, long-lasting friends who don't possess a certain level of homogeneity allows for a fully societal and human experience that two-thirds of the population will never have.

Thinking in a business sense, true friends are partners. They are in each other's lives for a reason, and both parties receive something of value from having and maintaining the relationship. It will involve a level of give and take, but there is a trade of currency without a doubt. Some of these currencies could be a caring ear, great advice, fun experiences, exposure to new ideas, network connections, competition, or just knowing someone "gets you." The currency may not be the same for both people. In fact, the depth of the relationship may not be the same on both sides. Having a mismatch seems less magical, but it really is a wonderful thing to know that the relationship is multi-faceted, complex, uneven, and still has the ability to expand and contract while maintaining connection. These fluctuations in friendship, the longer they can go without breaking, are a representation that two paths can be parallel and intersect, but remain distinctly their own.

    Friends have a way of amplifying your personality. They see things and traits in you that you or the rest of the world may not. They admire and exalt these traits. Things like, "you're so good looking," "you are a funny person," or "you are so wild and irreverent." These are outside depictions of your personality that you may have never self-discovered. They are something that you can embody and emphasize that increases your social value in a new way, even adding more of that value to the friendship itself. You are capable of bringing this out in others as well. As critical as this is for your personal growth and development, you have to be cognisant of its effects, though. While building this confidence, you are attaching this version of yourself to an external force, the friendship. If you are the wild and irreverent person to your friend, it becomes hard to walk that back to a sensible, considerate person on average. Your friend holds you to a standard that you try to meet. One of the differences between friends and family is spanning multiple phases of life. When befriending others, we tend to view them as static and a set version of themselves; at a similar phase as us, and we don't tend to notice our personal progression. This is why friends are naturally volatile shareholders. As you both change, the commonalities can diverge. After months or years, neither of you will be who you once were, and why would you want to be? It is very common later in life, you or your newer found friends will notice how your personality changes around certain old friends. It is like another person. It is another person. A past version of yourself, made and frozen in that relationship that you look back fondly on, even miss at times. The difficulty is not seeing that as a loss, but as proof of your growth.

Like a business relationship, however, you have to maintain your clauses and contracts to protect the business as a whole (that is, you). Friends have bonds; they can be strong, but just as easily weak. Keeping with the idea that our job is to protect and progress our value and, at times, our operational sanity, we have to be aware of the impacts our partners make. Few friends last a lifetime, and sometimes none. Sometimes a bond can hold you back. Sometimes one side of a relationship stops receiving the value, and the relationship becomes no longer symbiotic. Ultimately, the paths that intertwine now are going to two different places. This is hard for both sides, and a natural progression of human relationships. What is best is to see it, transition with grace, and not harbor ill will. Be grateful for the good times, learn and cherish the bad, and the people who were with you for those times. Take away the memories and be open to rekindling them with your future selves should the opportunity present itself.

One of the most pinnacle moments that I had in my life was forcing a shift in my personal relationships. In my early twenties, I had a tight group of friends. We were inseparable, some of us for a decade. We lived together, worked in restaurants and bars together, partied together, and would do nearly anything for each other. It was pretty great and a lot of fun. I never questioned our friendship or the fact that we had each other's backs. With all of us coming from less than stable backgrounds, I can tell you that it was the most secure any of us felt.

As I progressed in my college education, and it came time for me to make decisions to act on my goals of meaningful employment, financial stability, finding a spouse, and growing up some, I started to notice the stark difference in the way my friends and I saw our futures. Many of them were content with their life and their trajectory. I was not. I knew I wanted more than a life of parties and chasing tips in the bar. I wanted a stable job and family, something none of us knew anything about. I wanted to start investing in the life I wanted, rather than literally and metaphorically living paycheck to paycheck. When I voiced this, it opened a chasm. The mutual interests that we hadimmediately started to dissolve. With these differences rapidly developing between us, I knew that there wasn't a slow transition possible. I loved that life so much, the freedom, bonds, and excitement, and I knew that anything short of a drastic separation would not allow me to do what was necessary to achieve the goals I had in the timeline I had set for myself. So, I moved out of our commune. I went to live alone for the first time in my life. I got a new job that didn't rely on the connections of my past. I intentionally worked on meeting a partner without considering if they would get along with my friends. I shook the identity that I had been locked into by my friends that I spent all my time with, along with the habits and mindsets that came with them. Ultimately took the next big and difficult step to being the person I wanted to be.

This step wasn't easy or painless, but I felt a responsibility to have the hard and in-depth discussion with my comrades about why I made these decisions. As any breakup with someone you care or cared for deserves, a debrief was needed. I explained how I was trying to take steps to mature, find a partner, focus on a career, and generally start to grow up, because, fun as our lives were, it was hollow and time to move on. I won't pretend that they understood or wished me well. Many of these friends and I parted ways permanently. There was a feeling of betrayal that had entered the relationship. A feeling of judgment and imbalance. How dare someone in the fold question if we were doing the right and responsible thing? There were rumors and ill will that followed. I had officially and fully revoked my membership to the club and was on the outside. This kept me shut in for a little while, wondering if I made the right choice. My expenses grew, being on my own, so it forced me to focus on work, school, and getting to know new people. I deepened many friendships that were neglected, I dug into new hobbies, and I met new friends who shared similar beliefs and trajectories. All this eventually led me to meet my partner of ten years at the time of writing this. I can think of no point in my life where I felt so convicted, lost, unsure, determined, and self-conscious. I remain grateful to my previous self for acknowledging the misalignment of my goals and actions and the courage to make the changes I did. I always look back fondly on these times, but I also know that my life would have ended up drastically different, and I am not convinced it would be for the better if I had not committed to the change my conscience begged me for.

    The last Shareholder type that I wanted to discuss is who I think is the most important, and that is your spouse or partner. Your partner spans all the types of shareholders mentioned; they become your family, and one of the only family members that you will get to choose. They are like your teachers and coaches in the sense that no one will get to know you more and will see things in you that no one else will, good and bad, and will bring perspectives worthy of your respect and consideration. They are also your closest friend. A person to share adventures with, make mistakes together, and be there, supporting in good times and bad. While I do hope that this topic won't be controversial, in my experience, though, it always ends up that way

It has been shown that a key indicator of personal success is choosing the right partner. I like to believe this through my own exposure and experience. Dual household incomes are the start of that. In 2024, according to the Bureau of Labor Statistics, roughly sixty percent of married couples both worked.[15] Both spouses are also trending towards relatively the same amount of income in these two full-time income households; toda,y it is around thirty percent and climbing.[16] Furthermore, studies show that marriage produces longer total life expectancy, especially in older age. According to a study by the National Institute of Health, which studied people over the age of sixty-five. They found that being married will add about two and a half years of average life expectancy, and most of that is "Active Life Expectancy."[17]

There is a flip side to that coin as well. Divorce is devastating. The old adage that half of marriages end in divorce still rings true, with the caveat that second and third marriages end at a much higher rate. The average cost of a divorce is seven thousand dollars; mix that with the reduction in household income, and that is a huge personal cost. The mortality rate of divorced individuals doubles, with men being much higher.[18] All this is before you consider the real toll that this takes on any children involved, which, if you take time to review all that data, if you have children, makes "staying together for the kids" an actual logical move.

Choosing your partner with the remainder of your future in mind is challenging. Trying to estimate the future versions of yourselves based only on what you know of someone today is difficult. It takes diligent questioning, experience, and foresight. There is also no way to truly test these scenarios to be sure you get them right. All the same, they should be following the same paths to ensure you are just as good a fit for them as they are for you. In determining your partner, I have a few suggestions, as it is a unique and personal journey, but I may offer some thoughts to consider.

First, experience relationships. In your dating years, date with intention for the entirety of your life. High school sweethearts who get married are a rarity and often either that of fairy tales or tales of settling. You won't start to develop your adult habits and frame of thought until your twenties with some life experience under your belt, so determining the person you want to be and who you will become is too variable to bet on. So I only advocate for taking all your relationships seriously in the sense of not dating without the intent of being together as long as possible. Try to keep relationships for a year, commit, and demand commitment. There are a few benefits to being with people long-term, even in your high school years, and they outweigh the costs.

One, it keeps you out of too much trouble. It used to be called going steady for a reason. You build tight bonds, mutual friendships, and establish a sense of honor and social credit by remaining with one person. It builds a sense of credibility, confidence, and reputation in the sense that you both invest in a foundation, and there becomes a deeper respect for the person. It also removes some of the pressure to be accepted by the masses. Knowing that you are liked and accepted by someone and building networks gives you an ally and reduces the anxiety of trying to find a place to belong and be accepted for who you are. It likely won't work out, and that is ok, but it is much easier and likely to disrespect and distance yourself from relationships that you only see and intend to be short-term. So do not embark on relationships that you are not fully interested in, be honest, be respectful, be monogamous (even if it's serially), and try to make it work. All this in hopes that breakups, as much as they can hurt, have meanings and even mutual positive outcomes.

 Two, you learn how to manage romantic relationships. The opposite sex presents many challenges in its differences alone. Everyone is different, but there are tons of undercurrents that will flow through all relationships. Critically, how to argue with a romantic partner. You are going to argue and fight in any romantic relationship. When dating, especially, things will come up that bring heated moments, and experiencing them with someone you care about and are seeking mutual resolution requires practice. Furthermore, establishing and noticing boundaries in these arguments is a skill, no, an art. It doesn't come naturally, only from practice. Just as important, though, is how to be a good partner. How to read the room and get acquainted with the emotions of a paramour, messy, erratic, and irrational as they can be. Also, how do you communicate your emotions, and is it conducive to being read by someone else? Mind-reading is a magical talent and should be viewed as such, smoke and mirror magic. It is not something you should ever have expected of yourself or anyone. If you need something, want something, or are mad about something, work on learning how to say it without starting an argument. I assure you that it will pay dividends for the rest of your life, for you, your partner, and your relationships.

And three, limit your baggage. No one makes it out of their teens and twenties without their share of emotional scars. It is a universal human experience. You should experience your first love, your first heartbreak, victories, and embarrassing failures. In fact, you should try to experience these deeply for the experience and character they build. When you are young, you feel things more strongly than you ever will again. Chalk that up to rapid development and a boat-load of hormones that you won't get back later in life. Dating with intentionality brings meaning and valid excuses for all the stupid things you will do while letting you experience romance with guardrails of stability. It gives you more time to work through betrayed trust with lower stakes. It helps you see bad situations coming sooner, but it also helps you determine what you truly like and value in relationships. So have the crush, ask them out, but give it all you have and, like a connoisseur of wine, develop the taste and hone your palette while seeing these relationships as what they are, tryouts for the real thing. Knowing all the habits and decisions made in tryouts can affect your outcome, positively and negatively.

However, finding your partner is only one step in the journey. You will spend about ten years dreaming about your wedding, and then the fun begins, making it work. Warren Buffett is credited with saying, "if you want a marriage to last, marry someone with low expectations." As with many things in life, it isn't circumstances that define our feelings of an outcome, but rather our expectations going in. Having high expectations of anyone is most certainly going to lead to a level of disappointment. So managing your expectations for your marriage is crucial to its success. Your wildest, selfish desires are a solid first step. If you hope to stay married and happy, you must submit a large part of yourself to the other person. I don't say this as a synonym for slavery at all, but a gift that you should give and one you could expect to receive. A heavy consideration to the other in the sense that you can devote your efforts to looking out for them, because they are doing the same for you. Rabbi Manis Friedman gave a point that drives at the heart of this. In one of his addresses, he points out that "for a marriage to work, it has to be between a husband and a wife."[19] The quote isn't calling out some conservative simplification that marriage must be between a man and a woman, though he may imply that elsewhere, but no, it is a statement of the roles one has to assume to make marriage work. As individuals, humans are pretty incompatible, but assuming the identity of a husband or wife and owning that identity implies that at one's core, they are devoted to the other. I am a firm believer in the idea that marriage is a net positive. I mean, look at the stats, you live longer, you make more money, etc. However, if you get married with the expectation that the marriage is for your happiness, then you have set high expectations for the other. You don't know how to make yourself happy, so why would you lay that at the feet of the other? No, you get married to fuse your identity, success, and future with the other.

That is the framing, but what puts it into action is that from day one, divorce is not an option. That is not an absolute; bad things happen, and divorce is obviously legal and in some cases very necessary, but we in many parts of the world have made that more the rule than the exception. Marriage is hard; spouses will see the very worst in each other. Not just hard days happen, hard years happen, we change in unexpected ways, but what makes separation so tempting is that we are generally accepting that separation is a readily available option. This is why half of marriages end in divorce; it is hard to stay together and easy to separate.

While the practice undoubtedly has dark and problematic fringes in Western culture, arranged marriages have a divorce rate of around 6.5%.[20] When practiced responsibly, it isn't too hard to conclude why this would be the case. In most cases, marriages are arranged by the families. Families, wanting the best for their children and the extended families as a whole, who are much tighter knit than the typical US family, have a responsibility to choose a familiar network that produces tighter bonds and support. The communal need for stable marriages is a driving in ensuring matchmaking is successful. Love is not the key driver, but the function that marriage serves. As most Americans look at this as fringe and a cringeworthy taboo, it can't go unsaid that this form of pairing accounts for half or more of marriages taking place in the world today and has stood the test of time, producing better results than the nuanced romantic marriage.

These arrangements remove from the "Paradox of Choice," whereas Barry Schwartz, in his work, describes a situation where you have so many choices that once you make a choice, you can't be happy because you are never certain that any of the other options weren't better, thus putting any negative outcomes on you solely because of a poor decision.[21] Furthermore, it applies to the idea that it exists at a level higher than the honeymoon period. Again, appealing more towards the functions than the feelings. In many parts of the world and definitely throughout, marriage is a necessary function and one that has served the greater good of the world in many ways. It could, however, be thought of even as a cold and calculated economic decision, but it would require buy-in, examples, and support to make it work, something the Western and more economically secure world is losing.

While I am not suggesting anyone rush off to shift to an arranged marriage for themselves or others if that isn't within your culture's norms, I do want to highlight that marriage is not necessarily something you should pursue simply as a means of gratification or happiness. In fact, marriage is one of the most challenging adventures you could embark on in life. The benefits of marriage are economically positive, just think, combined income and expenses along with stability of normalcy. Marriage is also an investment in your long-term health due to the partnership and support, as well as the benefits of companionship, harkening back to the couple taking more care of each other than they do themselves physically and psychologically. I personally believe, though, that the ultimate benefit of marriage, though, is a driver to continuously improve yourself with the support and feedback of a trusted and chosen person with a stake in your future together. Someone who knows the person you have become best, can see and hopefully complements your weak spots and highlights your strengths, thus making a home unit that is stronger and more successful in life than either could be alone.

Looking at your relationships through business and economic terms stands the chance to rob you of some of the whimsy surrounding human relationships, and definitely not the most romantic way to express yourselves to your prospective partners. However, I have found that it is the best way to conduct yourself in relationships by realizing and participating in real exchanges of value and striving for mutually beneficial outcomes. We all need each other more than anyone would care to admit, but some people we just need to stay in their lane, literally and figuratively, while some we need to invest in and have invested in us. We all will have different levels of need and capacity to support throughout the phases of our lives when our resources, tangible and intangible, fluctuate. Therefore, we must keep a pulse on our relationships, ready to give and take as needed, to shed partnerships that no longer serve either party, and to be prepared to update our social contracts as we all progress. Some relationships are long-term investments that, to truly be realized, must have periods of dormancy and distance before returning. Some have an expiration date set at the time of conception. All these relationships have some value, though to your growth and development, and shouldn't be seen as frivolous. So I encourage you to maximize your impressions on your stockholders and seek those who can be converted into your shareholders. Invest in others to create a symbiotic network in which you are a key juncture. Most importantly of all though, be intentional and present with those in your inner circle, and these relationships, and don't be afraid to assess the impact that it has, knowing that the impact is larger than the interactions and you are a key role in that. If you bring value to a relationship, you can make a difference larger than you may ever dream, and sometimes that can simply come in its absence. It is all our great power and responsibility.

Know the costs

Why are we so obsessed with the idea of money? Nearly anything that ever gets done is done with some sort of financial incentive in mind. Most of us, if we think about why we work, jump straight to the explanation of "for the paycheck." Now, we will want to try and extrapolate some deeper meaning as to why, like the challenge, the routine, creating something, our families, or something else that makes us feel better and more in control of the fact that we need money. Money is simply a credit that allows us to barter in the larger system. It is the modern means to acquire goods or services. What goods and services, and the amount of them, is what we seem to attach most of the extrinsic value to. Thus, perpetuating the idea that the more money we can get, the more goods and services we can get, and maximizing our material accumulation. This maximum material accumulation can provide comfort, it can signal stability or competence, and it can provide maximum freedoms in some cases. So are these things important? Well, yes! Let's not try to find some high ground and fool ourselves into rationalizing that less is more at face value, because if you had the choice of having lots of money or having little with minimal tradeoffs, you and anyone else would choose having lots of money.

Therein lies the critical detail, though: trade-offs. Anything you will obtain in life, from money to inner peace, will come at some cost. You can break this down to the cellular level with the fact that energy is accumulated, stored, and spent. As an organic machine, you require fuel to simply continue your existence. Costs vary widely and even from person to person, as the idea that not all our currencies trade at the same rate, but no one can escape the costs of everything.

Running in tandem with the economic principle of cost is the principle of value. This is where the worth of something can separate greatly from its cost, despite their normal harmony in economic models. Generally, you would think a standard loaf of bread to have a reasonable cost in a stable market. Supply and demand would show that there is a plentiful supply of bread and a consistent need for it. However, imagine that in that scenario, you are starving. The value of that bread is much higher at that moment for you than for the person standing next to you on the aisle who didn't break the cardinal rule of not going shopping hungry. Your need for that bread is higher than the market average at that moment, allowing you to see the maximum value in the bread.

Contrariwise, imagine a stock. You bought it for one dollar on a whim and decided to hold it for a while. The market does what it does and goes up and down. Forever, you will have the cost of that stock locked into one dollar. It isn't really worth anything to you as you can't do anything with it, and it only costs a dollar. Now, say that the market now values that same stock at one hundred dollars. That is a one hundred percent increase and now you can sell it or keep it in hopes of more returns, but now it has a value to the market that exceeds your cost.

The market values the stock based on the company's stability and prospects for growth. No one buys a stock waiting for it to maintain or fall in value, simply because they want to support the business. No, that is literally throwing the money away. We buy stock in hopes of appreciating and, all possible trading advice aside, when we feel values decreasing below costs and we do not have faith they will return, we will generally sell it off at the decreased value and assume the loss. These are gut reactions. Experts and seasoned traders in the stock market make or break careers on the knowledge and wisdom of when to buy and sell to perpetuate gains and minimize losses in a portfolio.

When talking about buying and selling stocks, the concept of value seems boring and intuitive. Of course, buy low and sell high when you can. Naturally, cost and value can diverge and anyone who has ever bought a car can give you that example. They know that a new car drops twenty percent in value from what they just paid for it as soon as it leaves the lot. However, these principles can color our entire view of the world, and we may not even notice why and how.

Subconsciously, we are always weighing the costs versus the benefits (value) to make decisions, prioritize our efforts, and set our goals. If you don't think so, ask yourself why you do anything. Any mundane task will have some value that exceeds the cost, even if it is just avoiding negative consequences. Why do you brush your teeth? Because it prevents cavities. Why do you work? Because you want a place to live, and it costs money. Why do you pay for things when you leave the store? Because stealing is wrong, and if caught, you can go to jail. It simply isn't worth it for whatever item you wanted. These concepts are formed in all of us from birth: how to function in a society, as we are taught and observe. Naturally, we begin to see life through reward and punishment, thus cost and benefit.

Sticker price is obviously the easiest to assess and predict. Many tangible goods are going to have a Manufacturer's Retail Price that provides the market anchor and the actual cost may vary from that, but will still be an upfront, stated cost that you can expect to pay from the retailer you are making the purchase from. Consumerist as it may sound, we live in a world flooded with advertisements, discounts, and availability, so finding the cost of any tangible item is generally an internet search away. That is, of course, the fast and easy way to do it, but growing up with little money, I learned early on to take this to the next level, building a catalog in my mind of the cost of an object in a standard sense.

The concept of price anchoring and being in control of it can become something of a decision-making superpower when it comes to making cost-effective decisions. Cost anchoring is simply the practice of establishing the default cost of an item in negotiations. It gives you a base to see whether you are paying a fair market cost for an item and sets the stage for negotiation, internally or externally.

Let's say I am buying a standard t-shirt. I anchor and set expectations: soft, fits ok, color, brand reputation (if you are into that), and quality. I take those items and quickly assess the market. I can look up ten different t-shirts of different types and from different vendors, and then see what those vendors charge, likely in the ballpark of five to thirty dollars. The free market style of economics, as we experience it in the US, has a way of putting similar items in the range of each other, more or less, naturally. Therefore, you should be able to hash out something of the average price of these shirts and get an idea of what a standard t-shirt costs. Let's say you land on twelve dollars for what you think a t-shirt should cost if fairly priced. There are worlds of difference between the very best and worst shirt out there; but anchoring to the idea that you can get an acceptable t-shirt for twelve dollars, you can begin to assess what features would push you to a price higher than your anchor, or what features you would be willing to sacrifice to pay less than your anchor, or even assess the latest sales to see if the discounts then are worth considering, allowing you to gain premium features without a higher cost. All those decisions are not logically possible without referencing your personal anchors and expectations.

I won't, for a second, proclaim that a majority of people think this way when it comes to many of their decisions. In fact, you may find that the majority of your peers and fellow citizens do not hold many anchors at all for what things cost at the register level, and definitely not on the level of total cost of ownership or opportunity costs. Most people have been either the person at the checkout of the grocery store or the person behind this individual, where you get to the point of paying and saying or thinking "Did I really spend that much?", invoking some mild panic induced by trying to quickly recall your entire financial situation down to the balance in your wallet and checking account.

If you have never been this person, I am both happy for you and slightly sorry for you. There is a level of budgeting that many in our current generation of people with constant access to credit will not be able to relate to. That of walking into the store with a set amount of cash in your pocket and a list, trying to constantly estimate the balance of your cart with tax against it. I encourage this for every shopping trip. Paying attention to costs and the options to optimize them to maximize the overall value and satisfaction of the purchases you make. So next time you are in the supermarket, play the game. Set the budget and keep track of the tab. Get what you need and guess the total before the cashier or point of sale tells you the total.

The long-running and timeless game show, The Price Is Right, focuses on this fact, where contestants are continuously questioned on the cost of household goods. The trick to this that I have always teased out that the show is highly reliant on the cost of goods in one of the most inflated markets in the US, so costs always exceeded my anchors, being from a medium-sized city in the US southeast where cost of living is generally lower than most parts of the country, but what fascinated me about this was the fact that it made me feel a little grateful for the access to lower cost groceries and households goods. It quelled and grounded my teenage wanderlust as I looked at the economics of the popular "move to" destinations. My dreams became anchored in the idea of maximizing how far I could stretch my money and weighing tradeoffs.

This cost-of-living consciousness ultimately led me to stay in my hometown. The local economy started to improve with what I saw as comparable entertainment scenes to larger cities with great food and attractions, while maintaining a cost of living thirty percent or more lower than most other cities I would have considered. Furthermore, I was able to set my career based on local industries that I knew would provide stability, but also transferability to keep my opportunities open should I want or need to transfer elsewhere. Were there trade-offs? Absolutely! I am also aware that my personal experiences and preferences drove these decisions.

I firmly believe that one of the most rewarding paths to maturing and making the transition to adulthood is to get out on your own and remove as many social safety nets as possible, so if changing your location is something you aspire to do, do it! I only encourage you to chart your cost differences first. As Jim Roane said in one of his talks, "If you don't like where you are, change it. Move! You're not a tree."

Where things start to go awry is when we do not properly assess the costs associated with the items and outcomes, though. Normally, this is not an intentional or logical mischaracterization, though. No, it is one made out of innocence and ignorance. Costs and consequences are not always forthcoming. That would just be too easy. No, they require some level of knowledge to predict.

Cost of ownership is seldom thought of in our assessment of costs for items, small and large. One cost simply comes from not actualizing the actual value of an item you purchased. One place where this concept is amplified is the fashion industry. While studies vary by method, location, source, and prejudice, we can roughly state the following statistics: We produce twice as many clothes per year worldwide today as we did just twenty years ago, bringing that total to one hundred billion garments each year, for a global population of eight point two billion people in 2024. Thirty percent of these items will never be sold and will likely go straight to the trash. Of the seventy billion articles sold, sixty-five percent of these clothes will be thrown away within a year of purchase, and the average American only wears maybe half their wardrobe. With any clothing purchase, a healthy metric to evaluate the value you receive from an article of clothing, regardless of the actual price, is the "cost per wear." That is to say, think of your wardrobe as a daily expense you pay up front. Invest in, if you will. So if you buy two pairs of jeans, one cheap pair that costs you twenty dollars and you only wear once per month, and a nice pair that costs you fifty dollars and you wear them once per week. Your cost per wear for the lower-cost jeans will be about one dollar and sixty-six cents. Your cost per wear is nearly half at ninety-six cents. Span this farther and assume you can get two to four years of wear out of a single pair of jeans, and you can see more of the long-term value. In most cases, you likely felt a little worse about spending the extra money on the more expensive pair, but they fit better and will have longer life spans or just stand up to more frequent wear. With some foresight and intentionality, having a higher-quality wardrobe that you get full use of reduces your annual clothing spend and can elevate your personal style.

Maintenance costs are often overlooked as well. Those are the costs to keep your purchases functioning. Let's go back to the analogy of a car. I have always loved cars; they represented freedom to go wherever you wanted. At 16, obtaining a license and my own car expanded my world beyond the walls of my bedroom, which was the only space deemed 'mine.' Now it was my car, I could live in it if needed and go anywhere… As long as my car would run to get me there. I didn't grow up with money at all, so obtaining my first car for a whopping two thousand dollars was a feat. However, two thousand dollars doesn't buy you a cool or even reliable car, even when I got one in the 2000s. I was very fortunate, though, to have an uncle who was a mechanic who would help me keep it running. He had one rule that he told me upfront: "Things will break and you can't always predict a breakdown, and I will help, but if you run out of gas, oil, or water, you are on your own." For anyone who has a modern car, fixing your own automobile may be a pipe dream without equipment, computers, etc. Furthermore, maintenance routines are friendlier than ever, but some things ring true. First being, that normal care and preventive maintenance are a requirement to keep any engine running. I can't say that I have ever left a standard oil change feeling good about the money I just spent, no, but I know that it is necessary as someone who was taught to diligently listen to an engine for sounds that might be indicative of an issue, scarred by the traumatic event of roadside breakdowns far away from home. Secondly, poor vehicle maintenance can come with direct costs. Bald tires increase the risk of losing traction and braking time, a seized engine from oil loss or leaks can bring some cars to a halt abruptly and total your vehicle, and brake failures can cause catastrophic accidents due to a failure to stop. These types of accidents can be seriously dangerous, costly, and worst of all, preventable. Lastly, these maintenance costs are often predictable. For example, a car that requires premium fuel will cost up to thirty percent more in fuel costs, and synthetic oil requirements will likely cost you three times as much for twice the mileage recommended between changes. At the risk of preaching auto safety, but with a dozen years in the field, I can attest firsthand to the fact that micro decisions will have direct impacts on the driving cost and experience. While the average speed of drivers on the road continues to increase, it is great to consider the facts that may logically persuade you to reduce your own driving speeds as a start. For fuel efficiency, thirty-five to fifty-five miles per hour is optimal. At sixty-five miles per hour, you will lose eight percent of that efficiency, and you will lose twenty-eight percent of optimal fuel efficiency driving eighty miles per hour. When you weigh that with the average American saving an average of only one minute per trip for driving in excess of eighty miles per hour, it is easy to see how the illusion of fast driving is not as economical as it appears on the surface.

Owning anything at all even has its own inherent cost, without paying anything at all.. Sometimes that cost is intangible. Excess, as we experience in the first world today, carries with it a heavy mental weight. There is a theory that I have found to be true for myself, and that is, each time you purchase something, you gain a sense of ownership over it, and as humans, we are hardwired to maintain an inventory of all the things that we own. You have to remember where it is, when to use it, what maintenance it needs, evaluate its value, and so on. The peace that you stand to lose when the hard drive in your head is filled to the brim with the tally of your belongings can be huge. Like in a computer low on memory will exhibit slow processing speeds that can inhibit the most mundane of tasks. Sometimes that intangible cost is simply craving more. I am convinced that collecting and hoarding is a genetic trait. As my grandfather did and his mother did, collecting items of niche perceived value has been an escape of mine. Collecting items whose value is proportional to the knowledge you possess of them is a sort of opium and a coping mechanism in the stress of unpredictable times. Where it isn't obtaining the item that delivers the dopamine hit as much as the accumulation of its triviality and the hunt for the rare and unique.

While collecting and hoarding, according to a National Geographic report, affects about one in forty Americans, succumbing to a feeling of scarcity and avoiding it is undoubtedly higher. For those who can identify as growing up "without," the stability in having a stocked pantry or feeling anxiety of getting rid of things is terribly tough to overcome. The thought of being without something that you may need can bring back feelings that may seem irrational in the current situation and paralyze us into decision fatigue or even long-term depression. I think this is exactly the instance Chuck Palahniuk described in Fight Club when he writes, "the things you own end up owning you. It's only after you lose everything that you're free to do anything."[22] Owning nothing is a utopian extreme in a sense, where everything you need is present, but you own little. This concept of "less is more" should be something that we remain conscious of or even strive for, possibly now more than ever, as we are flooded with advertisements that blur the lines of wants and needs, or even more so, the reality of our needs as humans, as we see things through the lens of social media and cultural influence. There is something of a moral accomplishment in knowing that you need little and act on it, or the idea that you can have the highest quality items, maintain them, and extend the cost of use to its maximum while enjoying the benefits of the higher quality item. Think of our great grandparents, they don't make things like they used to for sure, but the idea of owning more than a few good outfits was daft. They bought the best they could afford and only what they needed, then maintained them. It supported industries of tailors, cobblers, electricians, and handymen that created a supportive and symbiotic ecosystem of community while minimizing consumer waste, which was a minimal problem at the time, when compared to the landscape we find ourselves in now. Bygone error for sure, but many lessons could be learned about the things you truly need from these previous generations, where scarcity was always nearby and lavish waste was not a luxury most could afford. Where the origins of repeated truths like "money and possessions won't make you happy" took root.

Envy is where this seeking of comfort, status, and stability in the material ultimately takes us. Widespread availability and not knowing the costs of things leads us to see everything as attainable, or worse, needed. As we set our goals and expectations, we naturally lean on our environment and our culture to point to the things that we seek to obtain. We do this without consideration of the cost in many instances, seeing them as rights and privileges, requirements in a world where every desire can be met materially. I encourage you and us all to pause and consult a mood of temperance. Consider the costs of your money, your time, your future, and your very self. Do not tie your goals to specific material needs, because they are often projected to you from a cultural billboard. Don't let others tell you what you need. Look in yourself to define your needs, wants, and desires without the influence of a cultural gaze. Most importantly, don't want for yourself what others have, because you do not know what it costs them to get it. It isn't cool to show the sacrifices; all the late work nights, missed opportunities, poor financial mistakes, shattered relationships, self-neglect, and moral compromises it took to get the fast car and big house. It won't garner any sympathy to talk about the crippling debt that you hold and the anxiety you hold that you will lose it all while you primp around in your designer clothes. Instead, I ask you to consider the humblest possible life that you can attain and maintain that aligns with what you truly need and want. Seek peace and comfort without considering the opinions of the greater population. A commonly quoted anecdote sums it up, but it takes fortitude to put things into practice, and it expands past material objects. "Don't do things you hate to buy things you don't need to impress people you don't like."

Know the costs, assess the value, and anchor yourself early to the reality of your world so you are not left at the checkout wondering what you can put back because you didn't leave yourself enough funds to get what you need.

AVOID LOSSES, ESPECIALLY BIG ONES

Warren Buffett has what seems to be an endless list of short rulesets for investment success. If you look into them, you will see there are a few common themes, but one of my favorites, and perhaps about half of his strategy, could be summed up in his quote, "Rule One: Never lose money. Rule Two: Never forget rule one." In all his short lists, you will see this aversion to losing money. Seems pretty simple. If only! Warren Buffett has more chances than almost anyone alive to get in on the ground floor of any hype investment trends and will have access to more information than maybe anyone in the world to assess the outcome, but his approach for the majority of his investing life has been rather conservative. He invests in what he knows; he invests for long periods of time; he avoids losses at all costs. While he is worth more than $140 billion at the time of writing this[23] at the age of ninety-three, it is notable that he wasn't a billionaire until well into his fifties. Then saw exponential growth following. The impressive bit, though, is that if you look at a chart of Warren Buffett's wealth, it rarely takes a loss. It is positive, some years more than others, but it represents a true "hockey stick curve." A common approach to investing that you will see is looking for anything up in the investment space that boasts quick and large returns, and how to build wealth fast. While those opportunities exist, they come with an inherent amount of risk that would not pass Warren Buffett's sniff test since there is a chance to lose large amounts for the shot at large returns. He would quickly argue that there is a difference between investing and gambling.

So, how would you differentiate investing from gambling in your life? The market is wild. Things go up and down on a daily basis. Investing your time, money, or energy into something does not guarantee an outcome. Viewing the concept of investing anything at all with expectations of returns and not losses seems impossibly close. The difference, I would say, is time and intentionality.

Investing is aimed at long timelines. Back to Warren Buffett. He has said that "their ideal holding time is forever." If you invest in something simply to see a fast and high return, your chances of seeing fast and high losses are there too. Where stable long-term investments have seemingly small short-term growth, they compound and grow consistently and steadily, minimizing losses over any long period of time. Furthermore, it is only a loss if you sell it at a loss. Watching your investments tirelessly will emphasize every peak and valley in a trading day. Knowing where you stand every second is maddening, and a week-long dip can seem catastrophic, causing your emotional brain to rationalize a sell at a loss vs losing everything. That emotional trigger is the same one that you feel watching a roulette wheel spin and give you a huge dopamine hit when you win and a cortisol spike when you lose, and those rapid swings are a sign that you are not investing, but gambling.

Your intentionality is also a good test to trial your investments against. Why are you investing at all? Is it looking for wealth and windfall, or is it to serve a specific goal, perhaps not even a financial one? If you are investing, looking for returns to progress your material status simply for the sake of having more, you become less attached to the actual outcome and the meaning of the action. Placing a significant portion of your savings, or worse, borrowed money, to invest in something that you feel is going to double your money to give you the feeling of financial success is the impulse and short-term thinking that would land that in the gambling bucket right away. This is everyone who, with some financial success, the second they get it, runs out to buy a new car. It feels good and reinforces the delusion that they are good at making money and never showing gratitude for the amount of luck that actually played into their success. All the same, in the event of losses, they are monetary. Losing when you are gambling is transactional. Yes, it is money, and there are consequences of losing money, but the money is the focus. There was no intentional effort wagered, so learning a lesson and recovering from the loss itself becomes transactional. An actual investment has reasoning above the reward itself. It becomes the difference between a job and a career. It is the difference between short-term extravagance and generational wealth. Careers and generational wealth are not created overnight. They are harder to lose it all quickly, too.

Intentionality in investing attaches these efforts to outcomes bigger than returns. Investing time in people and learning can strengthen relationships and contribute to your overall positive experiences in life, and is often part of the motivation to pursue these things. Just as well, though, giving someone your time or learning something that in the end proves frivolous does not equate to a net loss. There was an experience there, a connection. Something in the journey that produced value, not at all tied to the outcome. That is the essence of investing, the intentionality. If I invested a thousand dollars each month for my twenty-five-year career and expected an average return of nine percent, I could expect a total portfolio value of about a million dollars for retirement. That gives me what I need to start planning and envisioning what my annual income and lifestyle could be. Let's say, though, the market takes a long-term slump, unlike anything we have ever seen, and my average annual return is cut in half; well then, my portfolio will look more like half a million at the end of that term. Does that change what my retirement looks like? Absolutely, but it should not change my retirement. My plans and expectations would slowly be adjusting, along with all my peers in the market. I may not have the same level of comfort. I may work a little longer. I may tighten up and save more, but the goal to retire is still there; the plan goes on, no matter the success or failures of my efforts. Furthermore, there was no loss, just not the gains I hoped for. Sometimes, that will be all life serves us: the hint of a silver lining.

We are going to be presented with millions of choices, big and small, obvious and not so obvious, throughout our lives. These decisions really matter. Even the sum of many small decisions that on their own are not consequential can have rippling effects and lead to long-term consequences. It isn't comfortable news to take in, and not something that we want to believe many times. Any time we, as humans today, make a bad decision, we deflect and attempt to shift the blame away from us and to something that was out of our control. It is much easier to blame anything other than ourselves for a poor outcome due to our decision-making. Here is where I offer little comfort. Ignorance is not an excuse, at least not a good one. Furthermore, for you scouts out there, failing to plan is planning to fail. We choose how to move through life, and the decisions we make are based on the information we have at hand and our ability to assess the costs and risks. Giving a formula to always make the correct decisions would be misleading and an overpromise by anyone trying to peddle such a system, so I will spare you that path. Rather, I want to encourage us to identify and stay away from the worst ones. There is a quote attributed to Thomas Jefferson that says, "The art of life is avoiding pain." While I do not think that avoiding pain is avoidable or even desirable, there is an art in trying to avoid it; take on no more than you must. I do believe that is an attainable goal. So we will persist in navigating the greatest compromise, choosing the lesser of evils.

So, "let's play a game." Someone has a gun to your head and puts a six-shot revolver in your hand with only one bullet in one random chamber. Your choices are to play a game of Russian Roulette with assurance that they will let you go after one try, or if you choose not to, they will pull the trigger of their fully loaded gun. You know that there is a third, unstated option, and that is to turn your revolver on your captor. For the sake of the exercise, let's ignore the decisions that you would have made to land you in this situation to begin with and think about this economically. If we do not play, there is a one hundred percent chance that we will be shot in the head. The chances of survival are less than a fraction of a percent. Option three says that I have a one in six chance (seventeen percent, to save you reaching for your calculator) that if I point the gun at my captor and pull the trigger that it will fire, and then, if I am a decent shot, there is a fifty percent chance that the shot will be fatal. That gives us about a nine percent chance of escape in this route. Lastly, you can just play the game and have a one in six chance of losing. That is an eighty-three percent chance of being freed. Notice how there is no guaranteed chance of escape. This is normally the case in all your decisions- no perfect choice. However, thinking about the odds, despite Russian Roulette not being a hobby I suggest at all, pulling the trigger on yourself is clearly the best choice by far.

Every choice has odds of the worst thing happening that you can see if you look. You can likely catastrophize something seemingly minimal all the way to the point of loss of life and livelihood. I find that in many instances, seeing the worst possible outcomes and what steps lead to them is much easier than visualizing the best possible outcome as attainable. That is partly because the best outcomes rely on some outside sources, a bit of luck, but the worst outcomes generally rely solely on you. There is tons of middle ground there, and to get from a misstep to catastrophe will generally take multiple subsequent decisions. There is time to course correct.

Personally, through my upbringing and many circumstances being far less than ideal, I took a critical approach from an early age and became blessed with a sense of foresight that I may not otherwise have developed, surrounded by better situations. I had a front row seat to see the adults in my life make difficult decisions and was able to witness and sometimes be a part of the arguments, applied flawed logic, and see the results of them. It got to a point where, by elementary school age, I was debriefing these outcomes and the missteps that led to unintended outcomes. There were some grave decisions that were made out of desperation, pride, selfishness, and ignorance. Things that I could easily look back on and see how it all went wrong. Now, I don't look back at these years or the adults that made them with any strife; in fact, with appreciation. I can honestly say that many of the worst decisions were made out of love and with the knowledge available at hand. Monetarily specifically, I know that it is hardest to manage your money when you don't have any. By the time I moved out and started building a life on my own, I was equipped with experience around creative budgeting, avoiding pitfalls that are hard to recover from, and an idea of the kind of life that I refuse to lead. I knew I had my life ahead of me and had just enough ego from these skills to assess and apply my potential, and could stay away from the habits and mistakes that I had seen made all my life so far related to success and stability.

In elementary math, you will learn early on that multiplying generally implies growth, but there is one number that, if growth is your aim, you should stay away from, and that is zero. Multiplying anything by zero will wipe out any remaining value. Everything we do throughout our lives is aimed at progress. Some things are small, some big, most incremental, but always progressing. You will have bad periods as well, where you see setbacks and losses, but the long-term aim is always growth. There are some things that can happen that are hard to recover from, and even if the loss isn't total, it can decimate your returns on your efforts. There are a few things that I have found to be the most detrimental to success and happiness, and they made their way to the top of my "avoid at all costs" list.

Potential limiting actions in the early phases are the first hazard. Around sixteen years old is when you start developing the characteristics that will follow you through the next ten years of your life. Anthropologists, psychologists, and biologists can give you a hundred reasons why that is, but it is pretty easy to see that long before you dive into your first doctoral dissertation. In the US, especially with sixteen being the legal driving age, teenagers are given a burst of freedom and responsibility not available before. This freedom is mixed with developmental milestones, allowing behaviors, proclivities, and outlooks that take root during this time that express much of your nature and start to drive you in the direction you will soon start speeding towards as adulthood rapidly approaches.

Parents, robbing your children of this freedom should not be taken lightly. Speaking as a parent myself, our inclination is to mold our children into the adults we want them to be, but sadly, we don't get to push that outcome, and the more we push, the more we may stray from the end result. This time is when the training wheels are off, and they are racing away from us, applying all that they have seen and been taught. We are watching with bated breath. We are ready to pick them up when they fall, but we are now spectators. Any pressure we apply while they are moving threatens to destabilize them and guarantee a crash.

It's a volatile time and an important time. Missteps can be corrected. You can spend some time on the wrong path and find your way later in most cases, but not in all. Some things you can't take back and can hinder progress when you stand to gain the most from your efforts, compounding. They say the best time to plant a tree was twenty years ago if you wish to enjoy its shade. A way to stave off regrets in your mid and late life is to establish this foundation and be forward-looking. Instant gratification is hard to turn down when that is the majority of what is presented to you daily, but it is almost never worth it. There are people who peak early, and there are some who peak late. For the best outcome, you aim to peak when your potential for gains is the highest and you can maintain the longest. Everything before is preparation, everything after is reaping the benefits. The only way you can manage this is by looking ahead and diversifying your potential. What becomes most tragic is those who peak in their late teens or twenties, and they pour all their efforts into maintaining a superficial peak that is tied to their beauty, popularity, or athleticism. These things are not trivial and can be crucial to positive experiences and development, but they are a training ground. The world, when you are at this phase, plays by a completely different set of rules than you will be exposed to for the remaining three quarters of your life. If you focus on these rules that are less complex and have built-in safety nets, you falsely orient yourself for the next phase. Make no mistake, your teens should be when you build your habits, your twenties are when you have the most potential to work hard and see the fastest achievement, but your thirties through your fifties are when you will pay for all of your shortcomings and start to see the missed opportunities that you wished you had taken if you made better choices.

In your teens and early twenties, the pull of sex, drugs, and rock n roll is possibly its strongest. That pull for some never fully goes away, but at this phase of life, it presents the most appeal as an escape from angst, peer pressure, energy, hormones, and curiosity are all at their peak. None of these things has a future in mind when partaking. Sometimes that is the appeal. There is so much ahead of us, and deep down, we know that we need to work and develop for a life of drudgery as we see it. Why not utilize the youth you are currently blessed with?

Sex. It has been one of the great motivators since the inception of life itself. Procreation is seen as a driving purpose of life at a biological level, and our system is wired up to incentivise just that. We got lost along the way, though. By my estimates, we probably started to get lost around the sixties. At the time. sex was once one of the riskiest things you could do. Contraception was not readily available yet, and becoming pregnant unintentionally was, and still is, something that could divert someone's entire life's course at a moment's notice. That kept a lot of societal checks and balances in place for both genders when it came to teenage co-mingling. This was also the same time that pairing off early on was the goal for the majority for a myriad of practical reasons, so the window of time for expected promiscuous behavior was relatively small.

Today, adolescence is extended. Children are exposed to the sexual nature of our culture well before their teens, and true adulthood doesn't materialize until well into one's twenties. Contraceptives are accessible at scale in many developed countries. According to statistics by the non-profit, Power to Decide[24], more than nineteen million reproductive-age women live in "contraception deserts" where there is limited access to birth control. Around 1.2 million of those women live in a county without a health center. Given that the population of this age range in the US is about seventy-two and a half million. Therefore, we could conclude that about seventy-five percent of women are outside of those areas. Condoms are affordable or free in many cases. I will not defend our US health system in the slightest, but there are constant efforts to close this gap, and contraception of some type is attainable to most everyone in the first world. However, I don't see contraception as the major issue. In fact, between 1991 and 2021, teen pregnancy has fallen from six percent of teens getting pregnant to just over one percent.[25]

    Having children outside of marriage is one outcome that will alter your and your family's life course and is one of the earliest major mistakes to avoid. While to the child, "mistake" may be a poor choice of words. The birth of a child is no mistake of the universe. However, coming from someone who is a product of a teen pregnancy, I can tell you that it is a mistake on the parents' part. As in, the instance of giving birth was not intended, planned, or preferable. This is not any reflection on the child, nor does it lessen the capacity for love of the parents. In many cases, the opposite. These children and young parents have a chance to build stronger bonds, strengthened by adversity, and are more privy to life experiences and clear communication due to their less mature parents. The fact remains that this makes life substantially different and more difficult for all those involved. In the best scenarios, both parents can remain present and can rely on support from their parents to stabilize things. However, in many cases, the immaturity will lead to parental bickering, custody battles, child support, and care disparities that render the father, mother, and grandparents substantially worse off financially and interpersonally. The separated mothers and fathers will have significantly lower rates of furthering education and prolong themselves to the outer limits of the average age of marriage. All these things present very unique issues that take the wind from the sails of the bigger first investments in life. All personal development takes a back seat to the caretaking of the child, as it should. Nonetheless, early investing in oneself for anything resembling a normal path to stability and comfort can quickly become much more difficult than anyone ever plans for.

As if those prospects are not scary enough, sex is becoming riskier from a health and personal safety standpoint. Without sounding like your school sex ed teacher, sexually transmitted diseases are real, can be permanent. They are also easier than ever to catch if you play the numbers poorly. Since the turn of the century, STD rates have doubled. Just between 2014 to 2019, the number of cases reported went from 1.9 million to 2.6 million.[26] You can research the rates in your area, but numbers aside, chances are, if casual sex is something you regularly partake in, your likelihood of contracting something undesirable increases. Contracting lingering ailments will, justifiably, decrease prospects of future mating opportunities, increase lifelong expenses for treatment, and can ultimately reduce a person's quality and longevity of life. Those items are the foundation of a base for compounding.

The number of sexual partners individuals accumulate prior to marriage is furthermore showing a direct correlation to long-term relationship success, or lack thereof. A study by the Institute for Family Studies[27] shows that the number of women with more than 10 sexual partners in 1970 was two percent, and by 2010, that number was eighteen percent. Given a steady increase of forty percent per decade, on those metrics, we are roughly projecting that the number is nearing one in four today. In that same study, they found that women with more than ten premarital partners were the most likely of all groups to get divorced, stating that at the time of the study, these women had a thirty-five percent divorce rate within five years of being married. These statistics apply nearly directly to men as well, showing very similar numbers. However, the effects on men are different. Statistics consistently show that women file for seventy percent of all divorces.[28] Removing alimony from the picture, men can expect a twelve percent reduction in income on average, compared to a woman's nine percent[29]. Men also have a ten percent higher rate, on average, of remarriage to continue the cycle.[30] I am not suggesting either side is better or worse off in marriage or divorce. However, there are clear correlations between sexual behavior prior to marriage being a driving force in the success of longer-term relationships. Divorce is most often devastating for those involved; the process of and the circumstances leading up to it. It halts, or can reverse, many years of forward movement in your wealth and success, figuratively and literally. Taking steps from before you meet your partner to mitigate the likelihood of divorce, including your abstinence, choice of partners, and the way you manage your relationships, are critical to avoiding massive losses.

      Lastly, there is shame and regret. Sex requires more than a physical investment. It requires a high degree of emotional and psychological investment, whether we choose to admit that or not. We associate the ability to have sex without attachment as a sign of strength and power. As with most things that require strength, it requires practice. Practice in not connecting. Practice to forfeit safety. Practice to use and be used. None of these signals are true power. Shame is a powerful human emotion. It is the result of acting outside of our conscience. Shame imprints on us the painful memory of the event to help us avoid it from happening again. That feeling is quickly followed by regret, wishing we could take it back. These feelings have huge risks, particularly for men. Consent is a fickle thing. In sex, explicit consent isn't the most romantic thing, especially not recurring consent. The notion was beaten out of us with every movie or article making fun of a guy for repeatedly saying "are you ok?" or "does this feel good?", but that is what it looks like. Furthermore, we have seen true instances in legal systems around the world, where consent can be withdrawn due to regret and shame. We won't damn any of those cases, but the fact is that this is a real risk, and men are the ones who are at risk following regrettable instances.

Depending on your study, seven to fifteen percent of accused rapists are deemed wrongfully accused.[31] There are also about two hundred fifty thousand reported cases each year,[32] with many stats around the number unreported and those happening in intimate relationships.[33] These are horrible statistics. Horrible for the women they happen to, horrible for the men that commit them, and horrible for the pain caused by miscommunication and regret.

This is an oversimplification, so I encourage you to pursue the facts and numbers, but what I want to impart is this: Sex is a messy business. Be respectful, be careful, but the best way to mitigate these regrettable situations is by avoiding them at all costs. Be intentional with your romantic partners.

Reducing a great deal of the risk of unplanned pregnancy

and social stigmas for promiscuity, what we are left with is a more existential issue. Sex is losing its ties to relationships and reproduction. Today, sex is seen as a right and recreation, and we are only now starting to notice the issues with that. The issue that comes about and begins to become pervasive comes down to trauma.

Trauma is a popular word these days, with an increasing weight in its use. The dictionary simply defines trauma as "a deeply distressing or disturbing experience" or a "physical injury." More often, the meaning seems to tie the distress to actual physical injury. Definitions and feelings aside, sex can cause both types of trauma. The act of sex has not been one to take lightly in all of human existence to date, due to the dangers. Understanding that at every stage of life that sex has deep ties to our physical, emotional, and psychological safety must be internalized. A few things you will do present such a risk of regret, shame, and painful memories. When it comes to regrets, abstaining from recreational sex produces nearly none of the consequences, but participating in sex as cheap and commonplace is proving more than ever to have a high chance of degrading our long-term success and happiness.

Sex is an easy target, but habits around your recreational substances are seen to be accepted and even praised in today's culture. The truth of the matter is that it is habit-forming with things that are counterproductive to success. Drugs like caffeine (yes, it's technically a psychedelic), alcohol, and marijuana are legal and widely used with minimal stigma attached to them. All three set you up with habits that, when used inappropriately, cause negative physical and behavioral side effects. The caffeine will alter your sleep and mental productivity. Alcohol will decrease cognitive ability, increase the risk of violent instances, and decrease the function of many of your vital organs. Marijana will decrease your reaction time, physically and mentally, and decrease motivation and memory. All those points could be argued based on the person, but it is important to point out that the worst person to ask about the negative effects of addiction is an addict. You likely know someone who has a less-than-healthy relationship with one or all of these substances. You probably see the negative side effects more than they do. It isn't so much the activity of indulging, but the habits around it. When you reach for substances as a cure to a normal human experience, especially with regularity, it becomes normal. A bad day no longer triggers some time to think, breathe, and debrief. It triggers a drink or a smoke to escape.

Something that I found as I got older and shook the appeal of drinking, myself, is that it becomes hard to connect in situations that don't have a specific activity tied to them, and the most common of our non-active activities, a drink. It felt foreign to reach out to a friend just to chat without saying, "let's go for a beer." The habit of being a social drinker became so linked to my mode of existence and seemingly all my acquaintances that the idea of taking a walk to catch up seemed impossibly foreign.

Habits get worse with harder substances. It has been said that heroin or meth can become addictive after the first use. Cocaine becomes impossibly destructive and hard to quit. These drugs also come with an overdose risk significantly higher than alcohol poisoning. One of the largest factors in this is the source, and not knowing the purity level of unregulated drugs. You can never be fully confident in the strength of the drug and what else may be present in it. The reward of the high or heavy drug use never passes the economic test. The cost, risk, and reward formula never lends to their benefit. Lastly, the social stigma that is placed on this can bar you from education, employment, housing, or even freedom itself. I am not arguing for or against those laws and stigmas, but more so stating that there are some rules in society and breaking them has consequences, whether you agree with them or not. Willfully choosing to violate laws of any kind carries a risk that often exceeds the reward, and statistically use of illegal substances increases the risk of committing other crimes, being a victim of a violent crime, and overall arrest.

Rock' N' Roll actually may seem like the least dangerous of all the harmful pastimes, and that is most likely correct. I am in no way saying that you should abstain from fully engaging in music. Far from it, music of all kinds can bring the height and culmination of the human experience, and is possibly one of the best things that humans create. No, not the music at all, but instead the Western music culture. Like alcohol and candy, too much of a good thing can become bad and produce rot. Music, starting in the sixties, began to produce countercultures, and these countercultures brought with them ideas, attitudes, and styles. The music that we listened to became more than music; it found its way into every aspect of our lives. With genres like jazz, rap, punk, and metal taking the lead in music subcultures that had their own style and identity, which can signal to the world your approach based on your wardrobe, speech, and musical preference. I feel that we are past the age of the die-hard musical social movement, but the playbook has expanded. We are enabled to take hobbies or beliefs and build identities around them. Pick your cause from politics, sexuality, religion, or a hobby. The passion finds its way into every aspect of your life, from the way you dress to the way you view the world, and even heavily influences your opinions. Then, you brand that on yourself like a tacky bumper sticker.

This exaggeration and narrowing of your identity to an expression in the form of identifying with an outgroup, especially at an early age, can warp your interactions with the world. Counter culture, by definition, realizes that there is a larger cohesive culture and implies your steadfastness to go against it. Human beings are naturally tribal, seeking some level of homogeneity for predictability and certainty in their social interactions. Will a mohawk, tattoos, and studded leather jackets get you attention? Yes. Is it the kind of attention you really want? Probably not. If you walked into a bank and saw that person in charge, would you feel that they are the most trustworthy person to trust your life savings to? If you are going into surgery, is that the person that you want performing it? Likely not, or at least it would give you pause, simply because there is more effort put into vetting that person and dispelling doubt. You will find in those cases, the least amount of originality is what you want. You want people in key roles to be generic enough that you can believe that they are above identity and are focused only on the task at hand.

That pause, though, becomes problematic. The pause to evaluate someone because of an appearance has been given the connotation of unacceptance. It can quickly land you accused of bigotry or a "phobic" title, regardless of intent. The truth is that diversions away from what we have come to see as normal take a minute to process. Being on the side of the person everyone is trying to figure out begins to feel like a constant, personal attack. You end up in a cycle of donning your extreme garb every day, getting looks and comments on it, then wishing everyone wouldn't react negatively to you, then becoming jaded to others for not being accepted, leading you deeper into your counter-culture space, where you feel as if you fit in. This narrows your community and puts you in the dangerous feedback loop of not being accepted. The widely accepted culture is where things happen. It is where money is made and success is achieved on a larger scale. The wider culture has room for originality, but it has rules. To be a part of the bigger picture, you have to know how to blend in with the masses.

Aside from your social engagements, one key, going back to Warren Buffett's investment advice, is never to use loans to invest. Do not use money you do not have to try to make more money. If you try to advance your position without having the initial means to invest, then it really isn't investing; it is a dangerous form of gambling. It comes in many disguises. An example could be taking a huge loan out for a fancy car to put off an air of success. It could also be an extreme of the old adage of "fake it till you make it." This is everywhere. Many people do not want actual success. They want the things that come with it and, more importantly, they want it without earning it first; as if they get the prize first, the race will surely be won. By fully extending yourself beyond your means in time, finance, or competence, and not actualizing the means first, you stand to lose it all, starting with one of your largest intangible assets: your reputation.

If you can imagine taking out a payday loan to give you a one-thousand-dollar advance on your paycheck with the standard 400% APR, calculated weekly plus fees (two-week cost will often be about $150), then taking that money to the roulette table in a casino to place it all on black, you have about a forty-seven percent chance that you double your money. Less the fees, you probably pocket around $850 in extra cash. All the same, you have a fifty-three percent chance of losing that one thousand dollars, and starting a cycle where your loan is compounding at a rate of four hundred percent per year. You clearly did not have the money to place that bet to begin with, and the net good you would benefit is significantly less than what you stood to lose. Extreme as this example seems by the numbers, you can see how fast you can end up on the wrong side of compounding interest, where the cost of a mistake grows significantly more than the potential positives of the venture.

Now, I am known to like a day at the casino. I have a bit of a thrill-seeking personality and honestly enjoy the thrill of the wins and losses. I also know I have an addictive personality that I constantly battle. I always want one more drink, one more bet, one more hit of dopamine, and need to rely on my better judgment to wrestle me away. The best way I have found to participate in a healthy and entertaining fashion is this: treat it like an entertainment event, because that is what it should be. Fun and planned. I love a casino that will give me drinks while I play and take in the spectacle, but I always plan first. I assess and set my entertainment budget, expecting to lose it all. I only use cash and leave my cards in the hotel room, so there is not even the temptation to increase my budget. Lastly, I celebrate the wins and keep my winnings in my entertainment budget to enjoy the experience. It is fun, not an investment.

The last major hazard to monitor to avoid major losses and setbacks summarizes many of the other points and waxes over the entire subject of living a good life in its simplest terms: don't do what you know you are not supposed to do. We as humans complicate this so much with concepts around moral reasoning that far exceed the normal bounds of life, but the number of deep moral dilemmas that you will face is either of your own making or huge exceptions to this rule. Every culture and religion around the world, for much of history, dating back before the early lawmaker and king, Hammurabi of the Old Babylonian Empire in 1792 BC, has had rules that kept society going. Something as simple as "thou shalt not lie, steal, or murder" to the seemingly endless list of laws and precedents in the Western legal system today. What all these laws have in common is the attempt to protect and preserve civility and fairness, albeit questionable in its effectiveness at times, and to create an environment that supports growth in population and prosperity at scale. As much as you can argue the intent and effectiveness or fairness of the rules, one thing is consistent for both playgrounds and society: if you cannot play by the rules, you will be penalized or removed from play.

Illegal activity should be viewed as a no-go zone if you hope to build a sustaining and successful life. The easy explanation is that going to prison or having a criminal record will negatively affect your reputation and thus future prospects for prosperity, almost indefinitely. However, it is bigger than that when you think about it economically and how it relates to your very inner reality.

It seems like the very idea of the laws of the land is constantly being called into question by a stream of publicized politics, rampant scamming and theft, and even reduced enforcement of crime. A constant questioning of the validity of rules and reduced negative effects on those who commit crimes has led to a collective moral crisis in more recent generations. Online life and the presence of corporate monoliths have perpetuated the argument of justified or victimless crimes. There is no such thing as a victimless crime, and here is why. A crime is a violation of a law. A law is put into place to protect people's interests. Therefore, any crime is an action that violates those protections. The impact on the victim or the wealth of the victim in relation to the perpetrator is irrelevant, in principle. Scamming a little old lady out of her savings and livelihood has a huge impact on her, but all the same, normalizing credit card theft increases expenses on a company that has margins to make, thus increasing fees on all users and perpetuating rate increases. Petty shoplifting from a convenience store has a direct cost to the owner and their family that likely makes a very meager salary, but stealing the same item from a big box retailer perpetuates the statistic and causes price increases in a chain that sets the market value for items across the nation.

Lying is much the same. Truth, as of late, has become the most subjective word in the English language, with terms like "my truth" or "alternative facts" becoming commonplace. While in some cases the facts matter, I would argue that it is less than we all choose to believe. I think that we all have the tools necessary to guide us to a reasonable and objective assumption of a situation and make a conservative assessment of the morally correct way to act. It is easy to take a survey of what we think everyone in a given population is doing or reacting to, pick a side, and perpetuate the viewpoint. We will naturally lean one way or another on any given topic. However, things pick up steam, and in groups, we want to progress, so we go along with a few things others say that we question their accuracy or intentionality, then a few more things we don't really agree with, next we start to repeat those things, and before we know it, our very beliefs become distorted. Something funny happens when you say the words. You hear yourself say them and, all of a sudden, you trust the source more. You start believing your words, whether you mean them, believe them, or not. This is the smallest, but most pervasive thing you can do to yourself: saying things that you don't believe.

We often conflate the term lying with saying something that is not true. That is not the case at all. If it were, then a large percentage of provable science would be deemed a lie in just a few years. No, lying refers to your knowledge of it. Lying is saying what you know not to be true. You can't know it all, but you can speak against your knowledge. You can say things to deceive others or even yourself. You can make this work to your advantage. It is a known metaphysical and spiritual hack that if you psych yourself up, improve your self-confidence, or even actualize your reality by simply telling yourself positive mantras out loud. The same will work for negative confirmation as well. No one can berate you more than yourself. It is easy to dismiss outside, unsolicited negative criticisms when they do not match the narratives that you have built for yourself and reinforced.

Your words have power; this effect applies as much to everyone around you as it does to you personally. Furthermore, the little things actually matter. Small lies are practice for big lies. Lying to others is the precursor to lying to yourself. It is overall a great thing to assume that others have the best intentions with a healthy degree of skepticism, because we are all trying to figure things out constantly, but most importantly, the number of ideas and words that you encounter daily that do not matter to your grand narrative will total most of them. You don't have to interact, store, or even consider others' words and ideas. You can be the voice that corrupts

Avoid Losses, Especially Big Ones

the masses. Be kind, be intentional, but do not let the things that you do not believe be repeated, and allow yourself to create a distorted reality.

Throughout life, channel your inner Warren Buffett. Be relentless in avoiding losses and remain on the lookout for the things that threaten to set you back from all the progress you have made. All the positive moves you make are building something big, bigger than you. The bigger your portfolio, the more stewardship it requires to manage, and the more you become tempted to make a bet. The best and most stable investors will warn you of any sizable investments if you are looking for safe and consistent growth, due to their inherent risks. If you seek the thrill, treat these like you would a casino with respect for its potential dangers, and only with cash, you are ok losing.

I encourage everyone to consider their odds and outcomes. Avoid mistakes where the losses are too steep, no matter the payout. Much like a casino, there is a lot of luck involved in success, but many of the worst decisions we make are placing bets that we are not prepared to lose. Our goal is long-term accumulation. That takes sacrifice, and there is no easy path. If it sounds too good to be true, it probably is, or at least carries odds that are not in your favor. While avoiding the path of short-term pleasure and comfort for the chance at a better future will never seem appealing in the moment, it is the best shot we all have of better positioning in the future and the least pain and loss. As an advocate for wealth in capital essence, our goal is to optimize comfort and stability for as long as possible. Gambling feels good for a while, but the house always wins.

Educate yourself in what matters

Education has become something of a controversial subject. It is hard to believe, but I believe you would be hard-pressed to find many people who actually agree on what education means, how it should be administered, and its value. From this, the practice of education branches out and devolves into the political and cultural messes from funding and performance to curriculum and indoctrination. When talking about primary school, there are worthy battles to be fought on this front and some topics that should never be brought into the realm of possibility under the guise of caring for our children. How do you navigate these for yourself, though? You, as a student, do not get a meaningful say in the education board or PTA meetings. By the time you are in high school, you may know more about the skills you will need for the jobs of tomorrow than the teachers do. So, with these things in mind and wars all around you, what do you choose to educate yourself on? How do you decipher the good ideas from the bad? In reference to the information you are presented with every day, I say, to all of it... with scrutiny and skepticism.

I have to accept that I will always be biased on education. After all, I did not attend primary school. I was zoned for poor-performing schools and did not attend. I was homeschooled in the most minimal fashion, to where I can't truly recall lessons and would be reluctant to call it an education. One of the most pinnacle moments in my life was when my mother approached me at sixteen and gave me the ultimatum of my education: to join the public school system or get my GED and attempt college. I knew that joining high school at that phase would be unbearable, so I began studying for my GED and passed before my seventeenth birthday. I was fortunate to get into a local community college shortly after, where I spent the next four years chasing any degree, until I was eligible for three types of associate's degrees and dozens of useless credit hours before transferring to a state university, where I did the same thing. Choosing a college major is a pivotal decision for everyone. Most at 18, when you have had the education system vetting and informing you of your options is hard enough, but with no real influence or examples, and at a very fresh seventeen years old, the question of "what do you want to be when you grow up" is impossible. I will forever remain grateful for the way my education transpired. The depravity, freedom, and support of a Federal Pell grant gave me a deep appreciation for the experience and chance to obtain the level of education I did to start my adult life and career.

What this experience left me with the most was the realization that many forms of education aren't as much about concept mastery as they are broad application and regurgitation of trivia, essentially. Aside from science, engineering, and medicine-based fields, maybe a few others, when you are getting your education, it is more of a show of commitment to learning than what you are learning. Indeed, for the majority of graduates, it provides a way of thinking and a light form of pedigree. Your education lies more in the experience and connections you made, and the subject matter is less important and possibly even fluid. Again, speaking to what I know, while I hold a bachelor's degree in marketing, I have never been fitted or qualified to work in digital marketing or advertising, which was my original intent. However, in pursuit of my degree, I was educated in the fundamentals of how to market and manage products, creative positioning, and the pillars of sales and customer satisfaction, which changed the way I thought about business and influenced the way I interacted with customers which positioned me uniquely in my career and aided in my personal performance in customer facing and management roles. If you were to ask me if obtaining my degree was worth it for a career in marketing, no. I could have learned more about the craft in various internet courses available today. However, if you were to ask me if my time and money at university were worth it holistically, absolutely. I made friends and connections I never would have without it, including my wife and many good friends and colleagues. I also gained ways of thinking that are hard to come by without being fully immersed in an institute of learning.

But is all knowledge good, or even useful? We have found ourselves in an age of great abundance when it comes to information and also disinformation. The printing press, as we reference it today, is the Gutenberg press, invented in 1440. This technology is older than that still, but this was the printing press that brought the Bible to Europe and the world. That was also the time that we began to see a democratization of ideas at mass and all the good and bad that came with it. For the first time in history, ideas could be written out and distributed in mass, advancing thought provocation and making way for fundamental reforms of church and state. It still left some boundaries when it came to financing distribution. Mass communications had to be funded by benefactors who supported causes. The intellectual fields built in checks and balances to attempt to keep information as accurate as possible through peer reviews, citations, and the overall burden of proof. However, today, self-publishing is attainable by anyone. Fact-checking is a forgotten concept. In fact, misinformation is likely the norm. One major reason is that it takes longer to disprove a false fact than it does to create and even publish one. This leads to people today being able to essentially look up the answer they want to most any question, rather than a truly supported answer.

This concept isn't terribly new, but only been about a hundred years in the making and has shown its own form of compounding growth. As marketing started to pick up and boom in the 1920s, it began to be seen as a weapon against the masses, as its effectiveness improved as key players in modern history began to emerge. Edward Bernays is one of those figures, and he is also someone you may have never heard of. Edward Bernays is often one of the most credited persons related to this change and has been said to be the father of public relations. A nephew of Sigmund Freud, he began to quickly apply the science of psychology to mass campaigns on public opinion rather than simply product advertising. He worked on very effective public relations and propaganda campaigns to sell cigarettes, and numerous government initiatives that may be credited with fathering consumerism itself by laying the case and groundwork that an individual's wellbeing, happiness, and social standing can be intrinsically linked to their capacity to consume. That is also outside the work he did to test the effect of propaganda by playing a key role in the overthrow of a democratically elected government in Guatemala. I highly suggest reading some of his work to see how he laid out these playbooks for mass manipulation and how his campaign's influence impacts you today. His books are ominously named things like "Crystalizing Public Opinion," "Propaganda," and "The Engineering of Public Consent."

Many of these changes in thought quickly became entangled in the Think Tank space. You have likely heard of think tanks and people who work for them. They are normally non-profit institutes that consult and do research to solve big problems in specialized areas. There are some that do genuinely great work for things like foreign policy, military strategy, and domestic initiatives. The ones that are not always doing the best work are the think tanks dedicated to public relations and lobbying groups. These think tanks apply fact and counterfact to support corporate and political interests. Their job is to fund, do, or find research and experts to back up a claim, and simply that. Am I implying that the information is inaccurate or untrue? No, and that is the difficult part. Their findings many times can often be completely accurate and peer reviewed; however, their role likely ends there. It is like handing a child a loaded gun and sending them into a crowd. They are separated from the effects of the research they produce, as it will be handed off directly to those who paid for the service to present as they please to any end.

The Scientific Method is something you may have heard of before. It is rooted in the seventeenth century and is defined simply as an empirical method of acquiring knowledge. The seven steps in the Scientific Methodology are Question, Research, Hypothesis, Experiment, Data Analysis, Conclusion, and Communication. It is a pretty good model for approaching gaining knowledge and answers. As a consumer of knowledge, I believe you have one more point to consider that doesn't appear in this methodology: intent. Intent is crucially important to most things and is often not given the attention it truly deserves. While the road to hell is said to be paved with good intentions, that is more an application issue. When you read or hear any article, study, presentation, news, or any other piece of content, can you see the intent, is it stated, and is it honest? Per marketing 101, if you see a commercial for the latest clothes or widget, the intent is to generate awareness, interest, or action related to purchasing. That is pretty easy. Numerous tactics can be thrown into the mix to increase their effectiveness, but buying is often shamelessly the goal. Consuming studies or assessments is a different beast entirely. You may not know who ordered a study and why. You may not understand where a data point came from, and who has the time to check? Ultimately, though, if you are being presented with data, you are being led to adopt a belief. Leaning on the good intent of the scientific method, we tend to trust the data presented and begin to frame our opinion on the data or the facts being cited from a study.

    The most pervasive of data types is statistics. Mark Twain found this idea long before the average person was weighed down with the statistic that we are served an average of ten thousand advertisements per day. Twain said, "There are 3 kinds of lies: Lies, damned lies, and statistics." Statistics are insanely powerful. They are a metric that helps us to what the percentage of likelihood and outcome should be. If you are gambling, statistics are your biggest, and maybe only, ally. They help us determine best practices and gauge success against the averages. When statistics are taken at face value, they lose their usefulness and can turn harmful. A 2009 study done by the University of Edinburgh found that roughly thirty-four percent of scientists surveyed admitted to some questionable research practices, up to modifying results and withholding analytical details.[34] Furthermore, applicable statistics can be equally dishonest and misleading. Quoting studies that do not apply to the topic at hand or omitting key factors can make the true results skewed for opinion purposes and may as well be considered outright lies.

    A relatively benign example of lazy or misleading statistics could be seen in the health benefits of coffee. A study published in the Mayo Clinic Proceedings, a study of more than forty thousand people, from 1971-2002, found that people who drink four or more cups of coffee per day were "56% more likely to have died from any cause," and women were significantly more likely.[35] That is the type of statistic that will make you want to kick your caffeine habit. However, the study states that they did not control or adjust for differences in other dietary factors, marital status, and other socioeconomic factors in this study. You know, most of the things that will kill you a bit quicker than caffeine jitters. Another study, published through the National Institute of Health, conducted a parallel study with more than a million participants and focusing on a slightly older subset of people, found similar findings when uncontrolled for the additional factors. However, they pointed out that they found coffee drinkers were more likely to hold habits like smoking and a more sedentary lifestyle. When adjusted for these factors, researchers found no or inverse effects. Ties to coffee and diabetes are related to the sugar added rather than the coffee itself. While I enjoy a cup of coffee more than most, I wouldn't say that I lean one way or another on the topic of the health benefits or detriments. What I could say is that if I ever wanted to take a hard stance, I have sufficient and credible research to back up either opinion.

These types of conflicting studies are everywhere, and it is intentional. With the right people on the payroll and enough money, anyone can bend science to appeal to a cause. To sell a product or idea, gain favor, or simply to stay on the right side of the public's moral outrage, a study can be whipped up to support it by just asking the right questions and/or ignoring the full picture, and it is easier than ever. Channeling Edward Bernays, he wasn't shy to say that the general population was "dopes" or "sheep." The data, science, and expert opinions thrown at the average person each and every day are done so with citations of people with loads of education and credentials that would lead you to believe that they actually know something you don't. Chances are, though, what they know is the actual data and perhaps the full picture, but it will be slightly out of the scope of the study, and the consumers of the information do not have the time to check and argue the details in search of the plain picture.

So what are you supposed to do? It isn't at all realistic that you can take all this information in or be an expert in every field you encounter within a typical news cycle. Well, you have to be a skeptic. You have to root yourself in your actual knowledge. But most importantly, you have to choose carefully what actually matters. If I am an occasional coffee drinker, do the stats really mean anything to me? If I am a heavy consumer of coffee and am concerned about my risk, then I should take the time to read a few studies and develop an opinion. To do this takes a baseline of knowledge in as many areas as possible.

Establishing this baseline knowledge is easiest when you root it in language itself. Understanding concepts can be a large undertaking, but understanding the language used to describe the elements at a basic level allows you to be in the room as higher-level discussions are going on without being totally lost. I have personally found that a vocabulary strong in the basics of Business, Finance, and Economics will allow me to comprehend most of what I see on the news, whereas a loose grasp of medical terminology and engineering helps me with keeping myself and my house upright. Mix in a short-term glossary for philosophy and religion with a respect for foreign languages, and while I may not be the most educated on any topic in the room, I can converse with those who are and slowly advance my knowledge and expand my understanding across many of the fields that I know I will encounter throughout life.

One reason that is continuously relevant revolves around medical aptitude. Being married to a medical professional and being far from one myself, I can relate to anyone who glazes over at the thought of medical jargon being thrown around in conversation. I by no means suggest going to pick up a medical dictionary and start reading for hours, unless you want to get to sleep fast. What you will encounter is the modern phenomenon of informed care. If you haven't heard the term, you are either lucky or didn't know what was happening. Informed care is the event where a doctor presents you with choices for your plan of care. You have 2 options, each has different side effects and probabilities to fix the issue, and you must decide the course of action. This can lead to paralysis. The majority of us did not go to medical school and do not know the reasonable choice. This is where it helps to know the terminology and your own basic biology enough to ask questions or, heaven forbid, Google it with any rate of success.

It's the same with most aspects of your everyday life and lives outside of the realm of obtaining intellectual prowess. I would argue that it is more important than ever to have some sort of loose footing in all major topics. Understanding the basics of economics will help you navigate the news of booms and recessions, what to trust, and what you can do about it. Financial literacy helps you mitigate fees and understand your options in the market. Simple engineering can help you navigate your car and home maintenance, and potentially save tons of money by being able to read through manuals in an effort to troubleshoot and fix things.

The internet is full of knowledge. Never in history outside of the last thirty years have humans been able to look up the answer to any question and get any kind of answer in seconds. Not all the information is bad, either. But it takes a basic understanding of concepts of how the world works to truly decipher and utilize the tools at your disposal. It should take more than the first result in a Google search to find an answer. Questions that matter should require a bit of verification before arriving at your conclusion to trust a source. There is also nothing wrong with only loosely believing information when it is presented logically. You have to trust your gut somewhat, and like the complex ecosystem of good and bad bacteria that your gut is, it takes feeding it the right things to maintain balance. You have to root yourself in something of a concrete reality to give yourself something of a compass. Most of the time, it is simply ensuring that your own intentions of what you aim to do with the data are noble or meaningful. Otherwise, facts are trivial.

One of the most dangerous and seemingly common minds in the world, or at least the internet, though, is an uneducated skeptic. This is someone who cannot differentiate information and follow a well-executed debate. This is someone whose beliefs are rooted in ego and emotion when presented with conflicting information. Alan Toffler described this person in his famous quote: "The Illiterate of the twenty-first century will not be those who cannot read or write, but those who cannot learn, unlearn, and relearn." Mix that mentality with an ego that cannot tolerate being wrong and internet access, and what you are left with is a growing and perpetuating cycle of ignorance. You become the skeptic on the internet who believes every WebMD diagnosis over your physician's. You become the person who crashes the system at work because you thought you knew better than the person who trained you. These types of egos and unconscious ignorance will mire many of your own efforts as well as those in your proximity. It will send you down the road of arguing exceptions rather than rules and dreaded traps of "what-about-ism," where resolution or agreements can never be found because of obscure cases outside the realm of the topic at hand. This is the root of every division seen in this world today. To rise above the conflicts and set your own bearings in this world of information, be ready to learn, unlearn, and relearn. Be ready to admit that your information or reasoning was wrong or incomplete. At the very least, be ready to acknowledge the things that you just don't need to have opinions on for lack of knowledge or understanding.

A prime example of this is during the COVID epidemic, the World Health Organization had to begin researching an increase in poisonings related to intentional ingestion of household cleaning products and cleaning product-related poisonings. Their findings cited internet articles, specifically calling out clickbait and misinformation, as well as some black market drug sales, as the source of the information. This wasn't a US-only event. This was the world. Cases of people ingesting bleach to prevent or cure COVID, rather than attempted suicide, happened not with regularity, but even a small number of cases are too many when I assure you a quick search of "should I drink bleach" would present one with enough agreed-upon evidence that it is a bad idea. Another example of failure to understand and realize simple mechanics is the fact that about eighty-five consumers in the US die each year from power generators, simply from the exhaust emissions and running a gas engine in enclosed spaces. Each one is a tragedy, and each one is preventable.

It is easy to blame the people for not possessing simple "common sense," but that is a very easy way out. It has been taught, or not taught, for decades. In the 1960s, a high school education would include home economics, some sort of shop classes, and civics. Since then, they have disappeared from almost every school in the US. Over time, things also became more complicated and ever-changing. Vehicles used to be relatively simple machines, and now they are more computer than machine. A young man could expect his father to impart some mechanical knowledge or interest that would be reinforced in their shop class. Home economics would have taught you standard cooking and cleaning (and with a chemistry crossover, why to not mix ammonia and bleach) as well as basic personal finance and budgeting. Civics class acted to teach you how to be a citizen and maintain the political system by participating in it. These things all impact your life daily, and if left to teachers and parents, the expectation sadly is that this knowledge is "common sense" and is picked up through osmosis.

To make matters slightly worse, we are trying to mitigate this with technical solutions. Technology is infiltrating all the tasks that once required common-sense knowledge to do, and filling the gap that life-skills education is leaving. While this reduces some of the end effects of system breakdown by simply doing the work for us, it makes our future selves more vulnerable to complete disruption. We are building what I call "black box solutions," where we input some data and calculations that we are not fully aware of, and it simply spits out a result without showing the work. These black box technologies have allowed us to fully delegate everything from household chores like balancing a checkbook to administrative approvals that once required expertise and experience to render decisions.

A more egregious example of such technological dependence can be seen in air traffic control. An air traffic controller is one of the most stressful and demanding jobs you will find in the modern world, and there are lots of inherent risks tied to doing a good job. It is not easy. Most of the calculations and planning have been automated now, and staff have been reduced to account for the automation, but as technology goes, sometimes it fails, and when it does, it requires manual overrides just to keep planes moving. When that has happened recently, we have found that many of the operators are ill-prepared to do their jobs without technical aid. It is natural that there would be abundant slowdowns. Humans simply can't work as fast as the computers that are being put in their place. Humans are more prone to errors. It is exacerbated, though, by a lack of training, experience, and practice. Furthermore, humans are not robots and need rest. The job of an air traffic controller today comes with mandatory overtime, day and night shift changes, all on a demanding job that is crucial for the safety of millions of people traveling. So, when a system crashes and someone who is very tired and may rarely or never do their job without the system is put on the spot to deliver excellence, it is unfair and statistically unrealistic to expect flawless execution.

Expert is a term that is becoming more watered down as we go, as technology increases, and the understanding of how our world is put together decreases. The decline of experts is a huge driver in many of the workplace woes that we see related to corporate drudgery and the widespread acceptance of incompetence as a service. We have lowered the interpreted status of the front lines of many organizations when it comes to customer support and service in every industry to the lowest rung on the organizational ladder and see them as, more or less, replaceable. While management in many industries is becoming more divorced from the products they are intended to lead and the customers they are intended to serve. The silver lining is that as smaller organizations regain some power in the market, service, and overall competence begin to enter the sphere of focus. This puts more emphasis on the "doers" in the organization, and experience begins to be seen as valuable to organizational needs. It is becoming more commonplace and even desirable that key individual contributors can earn on the same level as management and grant additional security in turn.

Consuming data is fraught with pitfalls, but it should be seen as an honest privilege. We have more data at our fingertips than ever before, but with such privilege comes responsibility. The connected world is a tool and not a reality. Tools are very useful when applied properly and dangerous when used incorrectly. The same hammer that builds a house can be used to tear it down. My advice on consumption is to listen, build a base of your understanding, and be malleable and intentional with your opinions. Many decisions require simple data related to the decision itself, whereas overall philosophies require a broad understanding of concepts and their full application. So take it all in. Build your base of understanding in widely accepted principles and allow for updates from outside sources. Hone your vocabulary to allow you to understand specialized information.

I am not encouraging you to find "your truth." I am encouraging you to cultivate "your understanding." Understanding is fluid; it can change, deepen, and be incorrect without damaging the ego attached to "truth." Deepen your understanding as far as you can into a limited number of passions and professions, but don't take much stock in people who will discourage you from being a generalist if that is your inclination. To be truly wealthy in a sense of factual grasp of the world you live in, you should have something that you are passionate about enough to pursue a level of understanding that exceeds what the average person can quickly learn and apply. Something that you have stories and narratives on, things that you can help others better understand, as a way to show some surplus value. Heed the distinction that experts will take understanding in a deep but narrow fashion, where more diversified knowledge will help find new applications for their knowledge may add comfort to a wandering scholar. The expert and generalist need each other, and the important thing is learning from each other and teaching each other, which doesn't override knowledge or belief, but broadens the potential for advancement in understanding. While this is useful for your career, undoubtedly, it is a broader philosophy of being. Most of our relationships and interactions are simply exchanges of information. To strengthen your relationships, I encourage you to attempt to add meaning to them. Don't try to be the smartest person in the room, because the old adage of "you're probably in the wrong room" tends to be true. Instead, foster in your interaction a positive and honest exchange where you and others benefit from your presence.

How does this apply to your own journey of building wealth, though? Good decisions are made from possessing good information. Lack of knowledge makes you a target for a quick sell or scam. There is a lot that can be gained from exploiting the less informed. I discourage taking advantage of others in this way, just as I would theft. Your knowledge should not be seen as a tool to exploit weaknesses but to reinforce your integrity. Ultimately, the compounding nature of your knowledge and experience leads to wisdom, and that is potentially the highest goal, more than wealth and power, because with wisdom comes a level of security and self-assurance. Wisdom is not intelligence. One could argue that they are not even correlated, but one can beget the other. Our wisdom allows us to act with assurance that we are making the best decisions, giving the best advice, and acting to the highest possible good we can.

I will leave you with a paraphrasing of the Biblical figure, King Solomon. Solomon was King David's successor to the throne. As the story goes, God appeared to him in a dream and asked Solomon what he wanted from God. Solomon replied with "wisdom, to better rule his people." God, being pleased with the wish and motive, granted him great wisdom, and what followed was immense wealth and prosperity. Many of us, if given the chance to wish for anything and have it granted, would most likely lend it to personal gains of some sort, not acknowledging that a better self is an option. We would likely lean back on our current wisdom and see it as enough to progress us forward with whatever we wish for. Solomon, in the story, saw wisdom as the ultimate attainment that requires the longest amount of time and dedication to attain, and when given the chance, he chose that as his shortcut in his wish. He understood that security, wealth, and prestige could be attained through wisdom, where obtaining those things prior would stunt the path to true wisdom.

Some things are slow to compound and cannot be rushed. If success is your goal from a career standpoint. By the numbers, the average age of a CEO is fifty-four. The average age of successful founding entrepreneurs is forty-five. Age begets wisdom, and the reason these ages are so applicable is that it is a sweet spot where a person's peak knowledge and energy intersect to have the most effect. Why do ambitious young founders fail at a higher rate? Well, more than half of businesses fail in the first five years, and seventy percent fail in ten years. The primary reasons for failing are funding, lack of research, lack of expertise, and bad partnerships. In short, lack of wisdom, not ambition or even intelligence. Remember that life is a journey and not a destination. The most secure path to wealth is gradual. Don't try to find the shortcuts. Enjoy the ride, hone your mind, and keep compounding.

Plan for uncertainty and capitalize on it

If you were to look at a graph of stock market performance over long time periods, by decades, for instance, you will notice an obvious trend: there are ups and downs, but you can expect there to be a trend line pointing up, despite marked bad times and lows. Most booms are followed by busts, and busts are followed by rallies. If you look at the market, specifically your broad index funds, on a daily or even yearly basis, it is hard to see that. It is even harder to apply the knowledge that downtimes are temporary.

One way to increase your returns in the market is the tried and true "buy low and sell high" mentality. That is why watching for the dips of indexes is so sought after. This will work at a market level across funds that are looking for market performance vs company performance. Each market has something of a cycle.

Each company, however, with its individual stock, will have different cycles and can drop and never return, as business for one company can decrease, and not the entire market. This is why investing in individual companies is where the market turns more to the side of gambling. Let's use the phone market, for example. The market for phones will be the total demand and sales of phones; it doesn't matter what kind of phone, just all phones. You will have some major players and some smaller ones, but they all make up the full market of phones: Apple, Nokia, Motorola, even Blackberry, for example. The demand for all phones will remain somewhat stable until a replacement is found. Roughly the same number of phones are bought in the market each year, and growth is tracked. As competition in the market increases, some of the brands will sell more than others, and some companies may even disappear from the market. Sorry to anyone who bet on BlackBerry. When a company or product drops out of the market, the demand doesn't go away; it simply is picked up by other players, making the market more stable and the individual companies riskier.

Nonetheless, drops in every market will come. These drops are caused by speculation, performance, changes, as well as any number of outside forces. They will come, though. Same as in life. Our lives are more cyclical than we notice in the day-to-day. We have times of rapid growth and times of pure monotony, times when everything is ok, and times when it all falls apart. Sometimes we can predict and prepare, but other times we are caught completely by surprise. Again, one thing is certain, and that is that uncertain times are destined to come and go.

Being prepared is the only way to weather these uncertain times with as minimal disruption and devastation as possible. The old motto, "not having a plan is planning to fail," is one to live by. In the world of personal finance, that is the emergency fund or a rainy day fund. It is said that more than half of Americans cannot afford a one-thousand-dollar unexpected expense, and that number goes higher depending on the source and the age bracket surveyed. Gen Z is eighty-five percent. One-thousand-dollar expenses happen not too infrequently. It could be a car wreck, a minor medical emergency, losing a job, or just something you forgot to budget for, like a car tag or taxes. This leaves a large swath of people reaching for loans to account for. On most credit cards with a gracious eighteen percent interest rate, that one thousand dollars will end up costing at least an extra one hundred dollars in interest over a year's payoff. That's not to mention the extra nearly one hundred dollars you will be paying out of your budget each month to chip away at that.

Having and contributing to an emergency fund is the action you take to acknowledge that emergencies will come. How much you have in there is a lot of personal preference, but most would agree that it should be able to cover no less than one to three months of expenses. A good thing to watch is the job market. It generally will take one to three months for the average person to find a job. For the last few years, layoffs have been more common, and it has driven up this time in many industries. Any time without a job and savings to fall back on will create desperation and increase the likelihood of needing to take a job that does not pay as well or that you don't like, simply to keep from getting further behind.

I use the job loss example simply because this is where an emergency fund actually changed my life and the way that I operate. I spent the first decade of my career in safe and stable roles. They weren't the most rewarding or lucrative, but they were serving a purpose, and that was to gain experience and expertise and set me up to move into more fulfilling roles. They did that amazingly. I learned so much by staying in stable companies and roles for years. My catalyst to venture out was security. I know that I have a lower risk tolerance, and I needed to know that I had the opportunity to make risky moves without risking my family's security. A three-month emergency fund was the security I needed. I knew that I could go back to the safe and similar roles if things did not pan out, and I used the industry average as my anchor for that decision. So I set out into startups where things were fast, and my work made big impacts. I continued to grow my emergency fund to where, by my calculations, I could cut expenses and survive for up to six months without a job.

    Once I had that level of security, I could notice a change in the way I thought about my work. Until then, I had always been very conservative in my approaches to new ideas. I was very reverent to management and kept my head down to not rock the boat. I was a model employee, but I always had ideas or rejections that I left unsaid, and was disappointed when my input could have saved me or my team considerable grief in hindsight. I was afraid, though. I was not ready to flex the muscles of challenging bad ideas when they came from someone higher than me. Having the security to sustain a stint of unemployment gave me a newfound sense of confidence. I found myself thinking and saying, "The worst they can do is fire me." That gave me the license to practice "radical candor" and speak up in the interest of my customers, my team, and myself. As I was able to fully speak my thoughts, I became more effective in my roles, and I liked what I was doing more. I took the agency that I needed to do actual good work and not just what my superiors asked of me, and ultimately was seen as a leader in the organization. I stopped walking on eggshells and was able to rise above the fear of insecurity, and that allowed me to bring more of my full self to work and take control of my career.

When you can give your honest opinion, people ask for it. No one worth working for wants to live in an echo chamber. No manager likes to feel like they have to make all the decisions; generally, that mentality comes from a place where no one else steps up. Not feeling like you can trust your team as a manager is agonizing. Most times, that person is waiting for someone to simply show a little initiative with honest and good intent, allowing them to confidently delegate some of the responsibility weighing them down. Stressed managers are typically weighed down with things at the bottom not running well or producing the desired results, and simultaneously receiving pushback and little support from above. Improving the conditions for your managers by showing a bit of care and competence can turn around an entire department, organization, and personal career.

Muhammad Ali said, "He who is not courageous enough to take risks will accomplish nothing in life." Courage is easy to admire, and you should. Humans love inspiring acts of courage, but to temper the hype of courage, the plain definition of courage is simply "the ability to do something that frightens you." Courage can be as much of a side effect of insanity as it is bravery. Lack of fear can just as easily be ignorance. Who is braver, someone who unknowingly runs across a minefield or someone who sees signs posted and knowingly proceeds? If courage is simply the ability to move forward with something that scares you, it only makes sense to reduce your fear to a tolerable level. Or more so, defining what you are afraid of. Building security in your life does both of these things.

Security allows you to manufacture your courage. You can

minimize, in many cases, your fears. If you are not afraid of losing your job, because you can handle some time without income, then you can bring your whole self to work and do better work and not need to have a duplicitous personality. It won't always work out, but you can manage and calculate your risks without fear of retaliation. It allows you to set boundaries and enforce them. The best way to keep others from infringing on you anywhere in life is to be able to say no and mean it. No implies that you have presented a boundary, and if it is crossed, you have some recourse. If you do not have any recourse, then your protests are hollow and your boundaries are not enforceable.

Sometimes that fear is greater than money. Maybe it's physical security. Maybe you find that you attach more to your job than just the paycheck. Detangling deeper fears from the immediate loss of short-term security helps you navigate that. Fighting the deeper causes becomes easier when you can focus on the larger issues. Some problems require space and time to work through, whether that is therapy, a simple break to temporarily detach, or, in extreme circumstances, radical distance like a physical move to reestablish yourself away from things holding you back and causing fear. These needs should be heeded no matter the situation. The weight of these fears and imposed limitations can grow and fester the longer they are reinforced.

Incremental confrontation of your fears is a tried and true way to progress. Most likely, it isn't as big as it appears. Start with identifying them, thinking about them, writing about them, and speaking about them. These all serve different functions. Setting aside time to focus and thinking about specific things that worry you allows you to call out their existence and reminds you that they need to be addressed.

Writing is a tangible way of thinking. It connects different parts of your thought process and puts them into a third medium. It causes you to think about the words you are writing and then step back and read them, almost as if someone else wrote them. The person writing about the fears and feelings you may find is a different person from the one who reads it.

Lastly, your words are powerful. Putting your words in an intentional order allows you to narrate the situation. Listen to yourself, though, and don't just speak. Your words have a way of taking their own liberty and describing things faster than you can think about them. Speaking is where your own exaggerations and misrepresentations will come out. Who you talk to helps. It needs to be someone who will call those things out, and you can accept the feedback. It may be yourself, a friend, a relative, or a therapist. The key is that it is someone who legitimately wants the best for you and acts in your interest, and can see through the emotions exhibited and know your intent. Those people are not always easy to find, and you may not be the best person for yourself; even so, ease into those relationships. Vulnerability is wonderful to express, but it should be done with people incrementally and sparingly. Seek honesty and not just build an echo chamber of validation around your fears and emotions towards them. Not all fears are warranted, and not all emotions are honest or useful.

Your reserves are so much more than your savings and physical, financial, or emotional security. An amazing resource that you have at your disposal is your potential, specifically, your potential to resist, sustain, and reduce. Humans, like most animals, are amazing at summoning strength and resilience when needed to survive. Fight or flight mechanisms are hard-wired into our biology that allow us to summon more strength and resilience than would normally be accessible in times of dire need. Our bodies hold the ability to transfer tons of resources away from otherwise normal functions to the most needed functions to help you rise to extremely stressful situations. It is exhausting and can be harmful, but necessary in events when we are facing our fate to predators or situations.

A side effect of a safe, stable, and predictable environment that many of us have been born into and spend most of our lives in, free from mortal dangers with any regularity, is that we are not acutely aware of our potential to sustain and summon this strength. We are taught about maintaining our safety from an early age and are discouraged from taking unnecessary risks, from climbing trees and adventuring alone, as far as pursuing things that push us against the common grains of society and culture. We are taught through the abundance and availability of luxury that the basic function of the things we need is not enough and that the quality, brand, and design are possibly more important than the function they serve. When was the last time that you evaluated the baseline of your needs, what you can cut back on, and what you can realistically remove? I would argue that most of the things that you interact with and consume.

Take coffee as an example. Coffee is the most consumed food item other than water. It is consumed all around the world and mainly in the same way. There are vast differences in quality and preparation methods. Those differences can take the cost from pennies per ounce to dollars. Do any of us need coffee? No. The beverage and the caffeine it is known for are not necessary for us to stay alive and healthy. So if it is not required, but something we have normalized, what difference does the quality and style possibly add? Well, a good cup of coffee or a latte is much easier to drink for that caffeine hit that we all crave and are likely a bit addicted to. It is surely a status symbol to have the coffee house logo on your cup and the palette to appreciate the finer brews. Let's imagine that you lost your income and things became much tighter, budget-wise wise from where you are, which allows you to partake in the pricier coffees. Would you stop drinking coffee entirely if it weren't some personalized barista nightmare of a beverage? Probably not. You may just make your own, or you may buy a cheaper variety. If you are really down on your luck, you may look for the cheapest coffee you can acquire. You won't like it as much, guaranteed, but it served the function. A hot, caffeinated beverage like you have come to need as part of your daily life. After drinking that bottom-tier java for weeks or months. How good do you think your old order would be? How much tastier do you think it would be than it was when it was your regular order? You will probably appreciate every subtle flavor just a little more and savor it as the luxurious treat that it is. With any luck, you would have separated the luxury from the base offering and can see what the extra is for. After months of low-grade offerings, your baseline may have completely reset to that being your association with coffee, and everything else is a bonus.

  We can and should apply this to our routines often. Remind yourself of the things that you truly need and show yourself that you can do with less than you currently have. Keep yourself in a state of mind and a state of being where cutbacks are easy and possible from not only from a financial standpoint of living below your means, but a capacity standpoint where you can take a step back and breathe. Lifestyle creep, where your lifestyle goes up with every compensation increase you receive, is insanely hard to control. It is almost natural to want the biggest and best of everything, but building wealth is not about luxuries; it is about freedom and security. Maintaining a lifestyle that maxes out your capacity unnecessarily produces fear and will erode your peace day by day. Knowing you are free to fail, to take a step back, or to simply change is the type of freedom you can only allot yourself, and no one else can give it.

But uncertainty also brings opportunity. In times of scarcity, available resources have the highest value. This applies to simple supply and demand. Demand is not made up solely of need or desire, but of purchasing power. When the stock market drops, losses occur. The value of millions of shareholders is currently showing a loss, and this has decreased their buying power. When the majority of your resources are tied up in assets that are dropping in price, you are feeling the pain of the market, and things are pretty grim. In most cases, if you are looking to sell, you will wait for the market to rebound to allow you to sell at the lowest possible loss. After all, you make money by buying low and selling high, and not the other way around. When the value of all assets is at its lowest, if you have cash on hand to buy, it is like catching a clearance sale at your favorite retailer. You can acquire more at a lower rate and with the costs at a perceived temporary low. This is why those with money do significantly better in downturns. They have the cash on hand to buy at the lowest while everyone is reeling from all their money being tied up in assets that are currently showing a loss, and see the faster and more significant returns as things return to normal. They know the market is cyclical and, at scale, the market

Plan for Uncertainty and Capitalize on it

rises and falls.

So why don't you do the same things in your life? You will likely have many opportunities in your life that have a chance to get involved at critical times to maximize returns or impact, but it will require that you have the resources on hand to capitalize. You will need to have the ability to allocate time, mental bandwidth, or financial resources, or get in on the opportunity. Do you have any on hand?

If you have a friend or family member who falls ill, one of the worst things that can happen is for that person to be alone, feeling as if no one thinks about them or cares enough to lend a hand. It is isolating and discouraging. Having the ability to contribute time and attention in that moment of need offers significantly more impact than at other times, based on that need. It is easy to think that someone else will help, and there are others more able to assist than you, but this disregards the impact that you would inherently have on those whose needs it would normally fall to. If you were to think of this kind of action in purely selfish terms, let's say that person were to pass away. The guilt and regret associated with not being with those we love in their final days has a way of haunting us. Missing those last days because you have a meeting at work or something, otherwise trivial considering the circumstances, will be remembered in so many memories left of that person, tarnishing the good times with the wishes that you would have done things differently. Budget for the time. Deaths alone in homes and hospitals are becoming more common all the time. The final days present so much clarity and help ground us in our very human experiences.

Perhaps an opportunity comes your way. In my experience, there is no such thing as a no-brainer good opportunity. They still require some level of sacrifice, risk, or investment. A new job that pays significantly more and the work seems comparable, well, changing jobs in your career is not easy. You will and likely should ask: Why does the new role pay more? Are they accurately representing the job? Am I underpaid where I am, and is my current role bad? Is it worth making the change at this time and embarking on a journey that will introduce some instability? The new role may be the best option in all regards, but being able to make that move confidently and feel secure in times of uncertainty helps make those decisions clearer and less emotional. You can quickly assess your safety nets. Your emergency funds, if it all goes wrong, your resume, and your career performance, to assess how fast you could secure other jobs out there. If you have a spouse or family who depend on you, do they understand the risk of more work and stress of transitioning, and are they ready to support your efforts? All these things are their own type of savings accounts that you should be paying into all the time to build up reserves to have on hand and allow you to invest in opportunities when they arise. If any or all of your key relationships are barely getting by due to neglect, you may not have the reserves for change or extra effort. If you have neglected your job, career, and ultimately your relationship to the job market, it may not be as easy to take a career risk. If you have been so busy that your home life is stressed, then you may not have the support to put more stress into the relationship by introducing change and uncertainty. Having the reserves that you can cash in on for all your key investment areas is not just about a state of maintaining or planning for the worst; it really is about being always ready to receive good things that life throws your way.

There is a story that appears in the Torah and the Old

Plan for Uncertainty and Capitalize on it

Testament where a poor widow needed money to pay off a debt, but she had no money, just a little olive oil. She went to see the prophet, Elisha, and he told her to gather all the jars she and her sons could find and fill them from the jar of oil that she had. They collected as many jars as they could, and the oil continued to flow and fill each of them until the woman asked for another jar, and her sons told her there were no more jars, and they had nowhere to put any more oil. At that point, the oil stopped flowing, and Elisha told her that she should sell the oil, and she should have enough money to pay her debts and not have to worry about having enough food or a place to live.

One of the most compelling commentaries I have heard on that passage came in a talk where a Rabbi states that the oil didn't stop because more couldn't be produced. The blessing could have gone on, but it stopped because the family agreed that they had nowhere else to put any more oil. The universe does not like waste, and God does not want to give us more than we can handle. The takeaway and why that story has stuck with me is that we must continue to not only keep our cup empty and leave room for it to be filled, whether that is with knowledge, love and attention, financial capacity, or responsibility. At the same time, ensure that you have the most capacity possible to receive the gifts of life. This means creating and maintaining more capacity than you are currently using.

I cannot say enough about the difference I have seen in myself and others once a conscious effort to maintain liquid reserves in efforts to manage uncertain times has been made. It provides a level of peace that is invaluable and opens doors for opportunity and growth in every aspect of one's life. In a world that now revolves around credit, which pushes the cost into the future, I think we have lost the meaning of what savings are for. It's more than retirement; it is more than being able to make large purchases without debt; it's more than being able to handle unexpected expenses. It is a true growth vessel. By reducing our fears and adding capacity to capitalize on the good that the universe presents us, maintaining reserves in all our lives is critical to our peace, our stability, and our impact in life. A general rule that I have held since I was young was that being a man, or a responsible adult, regardless of gender, as I have come to view it, is simply about producing more than you consume. As I have applied this, I have realized that it is not only to provide for those around you, it is to provide and sustain yourself. You will be hit with setbacks. You will have your confidence shaken, you will want to take steps back at times, and you will be presented with fantastic opportunities that will require risk and investment. The way you plan for these things is to "make hay while the sun shines." Always be building your reserves, storing your resources, and being ready for times of scarcity, so when these times come, you can approach them with clarity and not emotion, with confidence and not fear. So start today, build your rainy day fund. It is the easiest place to start. Save a little and experience the weight of life, and get a little lighter with every dollar. Imagine that the elephant in your life is resting on top of you and keeping you down. Now, imagine every dollar that you have set aside gives you the strength to lift an extra pound. Build up some strength to move the elephant, and then you can train it to help you move obstacles in your way.

TRY TO KEEP THINGS SIMPLE

Harold Pollack has a quote and a book that took root in the personal finance industry, which reads, "All the financial advice you need is available for free in the library, and you can fit it on an index card." His book is aptly named "The Index Card: Why Personal Finance Doesn't Have to Be Complicated."[36] This falls in the same vein as Einstein's famous quote, "If you can't explain it simply, you don't understand it well enough." There are tons of books, experts, and services that can help you deep dive into any aspect of finance, philosophy, or your own psychology, but the truth is that not everyone is interested in these things, and why should they be? If they are not passionate about them, and there isn't a problem. While these three things are pillars to who we are and how we hope to live, being an expert in any of these fields, quite frankly, is not necessary and can even cause significant discomfort and meaningless interruption of contentment. The irony is not lost on the person writing a book, but yes, sometimes less is more.

Intention and reasoning are the keys to a simple and

sustaining life philosophy and optimizing your life experience. Why we do things is almost always more important than what we do, and if we aim to act with solid reasoning, then we normally can avoid major mishaps. Where you can go wrong, though, is not having the conviction to guide your intentions or the knowledge to apply reason. These are developed and honed, but must be built on a solid foundation. You have to have confidence in them, though. You have to have confidence in yourself. Consistency helps with that. Knowing what you stand for, how you will likely react to situations, and a grasp of the world that keeps things relatively predictable all help this confidence. You have all this at some level; your assessments may not be perfect, but with some thought, you will be able to answer these questions. To wrap this in a nice package, we should be able to present ourselves as wholly as we can to the world and ourselves, clearly and concisely.

Elevator pitches are an underrated and powerful tool in sales. They are designed and rehearsed to offer an entire sales pitch in the time that you would normally have in an elevator. Imagine you have a product or idea, you may find yourself in the elevator with a busy executive who has the power to buy on the spot. Going through gatekeepers, scheduling meetings and demos are difficult, but you have thirty seconds to go through the whole product right now. How do you craft your pitch? Quickly, thoroughly, and compelling. An Elevator pitch has five elements: a quick introduction, the problem statement, the solution you offer, the unique selling or value proposition, and the call to action. Getting all that into a pitch that lasts less than a minute and leaves an impression requires a few things. It requires an understanding of the problem and its impact on that person, as well as a deep understanding of your product. It also requires confidence. Not just for the courage to speak to this person, but a genuine confidence in what you are selling and its ability to add value and solve the problem. A professor and sales coach once told me, "You can fake a lot of things, but you can't fake sincerity." People can see past a nervous demeanor or an obvious sense of pressure and urgency, but if you do not believe in what you are presenting, any savvy person can sense that immediately, and your pitch is over before it starts.

You deliver your pitch every day, whether you realize it or not. You deliver it when you wake up and get dressed for the day; you deliver it when you meet new people; you deliver it through your work; and you deliver it when you think about your day as it draws to an end. You are constantly putting off a signal of whether you understand what problems you face and what problems you solve. You are also in a constant state of building your unique selling proposition, which is the thing that you have that no one else does. It could be as simple as a mix of what knowledge and experience you have, paired with your delivery, because no one will have that configuration. The question is, how is your presentation? If someone were to ask the dreaded interview question: How do you deliver it? When you get a chance to introduce yourself, what things do you find it important to convey to make you compelling and worth talking to? Most importantly, whatever that answer is for you, are you being sincere? Elevator pitches in sales and life must be rehearsed, personalized, and updated regularly. The worst elevator pitches are read from a cue card; they are cold and impersonal, almost robotic, and definitely not able to convey the warmth of honest human interaction. It is a script, written by someone else who, passionate as they may be, cannot be replicated as intended.

Keeping things simple for your audience is a deep compliment. It says, "I think you are smart enough to connect the dots and do not need all the small details, and if you have questions, you'll ask." The Navy in the sixties coined the K.I.S.S. principle for "keep it simple, stupid" (or any other polite rendition that you may hear) in efforts to cut through unnecessary details explaining known concepts to get to the action items. It keeps us from oversharing and unintentionally talking down to people by offering them the courtesy of the assumption of mutual understanding and a shorter time to the point.

We should aim to simplify any concepts that we hold to their highest level when working through our elevator pitches and even our plans and philosophies, we hold for that level of clarity, of course, but also to allow ourselves flexibility and the chance to expand the details and understanding behind the scenes. They say the devil is in the details, and normally, they are. Stating most things simply, clearly, and concisely with a little confidence keeps those devils at bay. Saying something as simple as "spend less than you make" is going to land and create more allies to the point than saying, "you should save twenty percent of your earnings," as Pollack's book suggests. That is a big detail that starts to question the proposed methods more than the initial intent. More so now than ever, it is hard to walk back, update, or admit mistakes. Everything that lands on the internet is seen as a permanent and unchanging belief held by the author. A statement with conviction and intent and a healthy dose of simplicity and generality, is hard to condemn your thoughts at a future date for less than precise details. Your brain is the same. It is amazing how we humans latch onto spoken words and are very reluctant to admit that we made a mistake and said something that turned out to be untrue or a misrepresentation of a held belief. Information and experience should update our beliefs. We should not only allow this in others but encourage it, if for no other reason than adherence to the golden rule.

So, in an effort to keep things simple, here is an index card with the principles for success in life. This is not the index card to success. In fact, I hope that you are able to take some of these items and add some more. I would encourage you to test these against your goals and experiences to offer deeper and more personal reasoning, finish the concepts on your own, and expand. Most importantly, take time to create your own. Develop your elevator pitch and practice the delivery to yourself and to the world.

Produce more than you consume

This is in line with the most basic tip for financial success, and everything else follows this. If there is one silver bullet to financial success, it is simply to save more than you spend. You can spend a lot of time and energy on good investment practices with your savings, but if you don't have any money after your expenses, then your savings will be minimal, and the returns will be minimal as well.

Keeping your needs and wants at a realistic level that you can sustain is a lifelong endeavor. As you grow in life and career, you will find that your ability to acquire money will increase, as will the cost of your needs and wants. Managing lifestyle creep through these times can be the determining factor in how you perceive and experience your level of success in the future. Most who read this will be in a better position in global rankings than they will ever give themself credit for, since their perception of success will be set by what they see those around them having and the marketing they are constantly subject to. True wealth, success, and prosperity can be found in simply needing and wanting less than the masses, living in extreme comfort and excess.

Being able to acquire more than you need is not only a benefit to your personal preservation, but it is the basis of setting up your life for the relationships that will add more value to your life than any material possessions. It will allow you resources to support others and the capacity for generosity that makes a difference. Saving and expenses are not the only budget buckets you should have, but one for giving as well. Generosity, after all, has a self-serving element to it. You feel better when you give, you show commitment and strengthen relationships when you give; and you build social capital and a legacy when you are seen as someone successful enough to share their wealth with others without the need to expect anything in return.

Having more than you need or use offers peace and contentment that is unrivaled in any other aspect of life. Having more money than you need to live, having more time than you have obligations, or even having more love than you need from others all open you up to utilize those resources in ways that benefit your future self while maintaining peace in your current situation. That peace is the pursuit of all the work we do.

Learn from all mistakes, not just yours.

There is no shortage of mistakes that you have access to. You will make tons of them. You will see others make even more. Mistakes are not a problem, simply the trial and error of life. The problem will be repeated mistakes or, worse, turning mistakes into hard-to-break habits.

The biggest benefit that you will experience from actually learning from mistakes, debriefing after, and taking them seriously will be to see them coming in the future. Many mistakes, especially big ones, have commonalities and thought processes that cause us humans to act irrationally and against our better judgment. Seeing these signs and having the ability to predict outcomes will minimize the number of critical mistakes we make and their impact.

Taking risks in life is very important. You should not avoid them, but taking wild risks that stand to cost you more than the benefits is not a luxury many have or you will always have. There will be times in your life when you have the capacity to take big risks, and there will be times when you cannot stand a setback at all. There, understanding the risks and the likelihood of success and failure is a talent worth honing. Furthermore, when taking risks, having contingency plans to hedge your bets and reduce the impact of loss will enable you to act with more certainty. If you must walk a tightrope, it is best to do it with a net; and if you stumble, at least stumble forward.

Understanding the risk and reward tradeoff, as well as your personal tolerance for risk, will serve you well. It will help you see pitfalls and avoid regrets. If you knew the risk and took it, then if everything goes wrong, you are less disappointed since you foresaw the loss as a potential outcome. Your confidence was in check, and your rationality was sound.

Knowledge is your understanding of information, and wisdom is the application of your experience. Use them both. If you want knowledge, seek education. If you want wisdom, look at mistakes and learn from them.

All information is worth hearing, but it is not all worth believing.

Anyone in the millennial generation and after will have no recollection of a time when information was not readily accessible via the internet. Today, there is little credence to the concept of common sense and understanding, as contrarian is the new consensus. Whatever belief you hold, you can find supporting opinions and even evidence or reason to doubt it. This leaves us in the impossible place of needing to develop our own concepts of how things are and how they work; establishing belief systems which can support a constant barrage of useless, questionable, conflicting, or even weaponized information and use it in a productive manner.

The answer is not to close ourselves off from it. No, we have to be exposed to it all to develop some immunity. You have to see both sides of an argument to see where the biases lie. You may never feel confident enough to voice or defend your opinions or beliefs on a subject, and if that is the case, do not be disheartened; be encouraged. If you reach that point, you have actually found the key to opinions in our times. You realize that you do not know enough to feel strongly about something, in which you can learn more, or the subject is actually not important enough to have developed a strong opinion in the first place, which accounts for an overwhelming majority of topics you will be asked to pick a side on. A few things that divide our culture today require individuals to choose a side and support. Culture, economics, politics, science, religion, or simply what is good are not something that we as individuals have much say in how they play out, but how we act in accordance with our beliefs without stating them is something that we have control over.

We all must hone our conscience and listen to it. To do that, it must be trained in the real world and not from any media or comment feed; how people behave, how the world reacts to you, by your own assessment, or how the science of life unfolds before your eyes, and your own set of acquired statistical data. If something sounds wrong, it probably is to some degree or there is some intent. Most importantly, if something sounds divisive or confrontational, it is probably time to disengage. The point of education is to help us improve and gain a better understanding of concepts to improve our life. While learning can be entertaining, if information is aimed at entertainment, it accesses parts of our brain that are subject to emotional engagement and cannot be fully trusted.

Take time to see, experience, and learn as much as you can, but do it to your own ends. Avoid learning as a way to persuade anyone to a point, don't pick sides, and don't identify with opinions.

Read a lot. Take what is useful and forget the rest. Acquire and use information only to serve you and your goals to better yourself, and approach all learning with a healthy amount of skepticism.

Aim to optimize for success, not to maximize success.

Success is fed to us in commercials, some by corporations and some by our peers. We often see and envy what others have because we only see the outward appearance. Looking successful is not success; it is just an appearance. Never envy the possessions another person has, because you do not know the sacrifices it took to get them, nor do you know the costs they come with. The image of success always owns you rather than what you own.

True success is found in security, peace, and contentment. It is found in not owing anyone anything, so no one can infringe on your security and peace. If you optimize for these things, you will lose sight of the material flashiness, and your needs will become fewer. Having a realistic grasp on your needs and wants, as well as knowing the difference, resets the definition of success and starts to shift it more to simply your level of freedom.

Freedom and success do not mean not having to work. It means that we are not bound by our work. Our work is done with joy and a sense of purpose, not obligation, simply to make money, whatever that work is. Success is not defined by an amount of money, an entrepreneurial path, owning your own business, or being your own boss. It isn't about making passive income and fuck-you-money. It is about meaning and balance.

Do you have enough and have security in your life and finances? Do you have that with it not taking up your entire life, leaving you with time for family, friends, community, and outside interests? That is wealth and success, and not a level that more than a large majority of the world's population enjoys, regardless of their salary and possessions.

Set realistic, long-term goals early and stick to them.

The best time to plant a tree to enjoy its shade was twenty years ago; the second-best time is now. Success takes time; you get to see some progress along the way, but you don't get to enjoy it until the plan matures. Let's say that you decide halfway through that you want a fruit tree instead of a shade tree. Well, then it is back to the start. Momentum is very important.

Understanding the direction that you want to go as early as possible sets you up to gain the most possible momentum. Complete changes in direction or even minor deviations can cost you precious effort and momentum. There is a lot to be said about staying the course.

Today, kids are given impossible decisions of making long-term decisions when it comes to their careers with little meaningful guidance. They are not counseled on options, goals, expected outcomes, or likelihoods of success. They are not given proper education on economics, finances, or workforce analysis to choose a long-term career. They are filled with a false sense of confidence and visions of material success and sent on their way, leaving them struggling to find purpose and meaning in the work that they do, and setting them on a treadmill to flounder in a rat race until death.

You can break this cycle; it shouldn't have to be this way, and it does not have to be. Set a plan. Driven by a why, start with what you do not want and set your sights in the opposite direction. Set your goal specific enough to make strides towards achieving it, but vague enough to allow reinterpretation, flexibility, and pivots as you grow and when life throws you curveballs, because it will.

Set your highest goals not for dollar amounts, material milestones, or a definitive end, but for the life that you want to experience holistically. A life that, when you reach the end of it, you can look back on with pride and as few regrets as possible.

Set your material goals as something to work towards attainable. Few things will rob you of happiness than setting unrealistic goals for yourself and failing to meet them. Allow there to be times where you exceed your expectations and times where you are falling behind and need to catch up. This keeps you engaged and demonstrates to yourself that your goal is properly set with the optimal level of challenge.

Lastly, give yourself space and grace to reevaluate. Assess your goals and your progress regularly, but not too often, to allow yourself some change if necessary based on your long-term situation. Your goals should empower you and guide your decision-making. They should not oppress you and hinder your peace, and be a point of stress.

Know the cost of everything and budget accordingly.

Budgeting is a key part of any financial plan. Knowing your income and expenses is crucial to staying out of debt and making headway in your savings. Not knowing what things cost makes it extremely hard to plan and budget. Costs are becoming increasingly hidden and not stated up front. Buy now - pay later, hidden fees, terms and conditions that are only in favor of the seller, or lack of knowledge around how interest and cost of ownership work, all play an important role in true budgeting that previous times did not have to contend with so much.

Just living in today's society requires knowledge of the true cost of everything. Whether it is as simple as how much groceries and rent cost, or how credit card interest and vehicle maintenance work, or even as convoluted as all the contractual language hidden in your investment broker contract, knowing these concepts at a basic level is ignored at our own peril. Worse, there are concepts that our youth are learning too late, like once you put something on the internet, it is no longer yours or if something is free, you are likely the product. We unfortunately cannot put our heads in the sand and pretend that all the systems we have put in place are there for our benefit, or that things are simple and they will all work out for us. We have to treat our age of technological advancement and economic comfort with the responsibility and respect it deserves. Doing so and achieving any level of success demands a grasp of the rules of the game and an understanding of the costs.

Not all costs you encounter will be monetary. Things we desire will come at the cost of our time, our efforts, and even our peace. Sadly, we often act in pursuit of happiness and comfort today and are not willing to endure the work or discomfort for a better tomorrow. We are sold the hedonistic concept of "you only live once" and maximizing pleasure by prolonging carefree youth as long as possible. I would challenge you to avoid the trap of fatalism and work for your future self, and balance your budget every day with savings as a staple. Rather than acting as if you only live once, I prefer to see it as, "you only die once, you live every day, so make the most of your longevity."

Happiness and contentment are not goals; they are byproducts. Know you're enough and live like no one else.

As Americans, the line of "Life, Liberty, and the Pursuit of Happiness" is a motto that is ingrained in our DNA, and we have shared this idea with the world. All too often, though, we omit the word, pursuit. Happiness is not something that any of us is entitled to; it is not a right, and I hate to break it to you, but it cannot be obtained, at least in much of a predictable and sustainable way. However, it is a worthy emotion to pursue.

Contentment is the precursor to happiness. The concept that we have enough. Enough resources, enough meaning, enough joy, and even enough happiness. Enough is never all-encompassing. It has an ebb and flow, and fleets us. Enough is not excess or absence of pain. It is knowledge that we have done the best that we can and have obtained an acceptable outcome.

Envy is the enemy of happiness. You probably have heard that and passed it by, but our culture has rewired our brains to envy everything we don't have. You aren't as good-looking as the models, your home isn't as chic as the characters on TV, and your career doesn't have the impact of the CEO influencers. You do not have as much as the people in front of you; therefore, you are not enough. I have said it before and will again: do not envy what anyone else has, because you do not know what it costs them.

As all the conventional wisdom goes, possessions and social standing rarely produce happiness. The things that you seek by obtaining status, money, and things are normally stand-ins and consolations for the things that actually create feelings of happiness and are more a result of envy and lack of originality. No one looks back from their deathbed and wishes they had accumulated more things, because they know that they are going to be separated from them when they leave this world. They wish they had had better relationships, been kinder to themselves, and done more good in the world. Money can alleviate discomfort without a doubt, but the happiness brought on by money plateaus.

Freedom does not produce happiness either. In fact, you may find that it is quite the opposite. True freedom requires some level of meritocracy, where you get more, you have to give more. True freedom means that you do not have the luxury of someone telling you the right thing to do. It is a responsibility and a heavy one. You have the freedom to make good choices and you have the freedom to make bad ones, and your freedom leaves you with the responsibility both ways. We conflate freedom and individuality constantly; they are seen as the same thing, but they are not. I encourage you to embrace the freedom that you have to be a part of the bigger picture, rising above your own self-importance, and offering yourself to the world as more than self-serving.

Your contentment is knowing that you are doing well. You could do more, but you have enough. You could do with less if needed to shift resources elsewhere. It is a balance where your resources and requirements are in line. Without contentment and your honest assessment that you are doing the right things that are worthwhile, it is very difficult to experience sustained happiness. That is why you should never set your goal to be happy, but seek balance and meaning, leaving yourself available to take in all the happiness that life sends us every day if we only give ourselves the chance to experience it.

No one journeys alone. Pick your partners well and mind your stakeholders and shareholders.

We are all part of something bigger than ourselves. We were not meant to act only in our self-interest and be a cell, shut off from the rest of the world. Like it or not, we all have a scope of influence and responsibilities to that network of people. If we choose to ignore the impact that we have, we actively hurt ourselves and the entire unit. You may see yourself as unimportant, but those around you will be worse off by your absence. Moreover, those you passively interact with just as you go through life alone sense when you are checked out and not engaged. They will reciprocate the sentiment and further your feelings of alienation. The unique wealth of the human experience resides in our interactions with other humans.

So to build these relationships, we invest in them, cultivate them, and with some luck, appreciate and value them. It all starts with our respect for the human network and seeing how everyone is a part of it, capable and eager to offer value and make the world a somewhat better place. Each of us longs for a connection beyond pleasantries and hollow connections in passing. They want someone to celebrate and grieve with, someone to serve as a confidant for their insecurities, and be able to reciprocate and commiserate.

We have access to lifelong relationships, some of which we do not get to choose. Our families offer us a great resource to give and receive love with the special privilege of some obligation. They get a chance to grow with us and span through all the stages of our lives, seeing more of us than anyone we pick up by choice.

We choose most of our relationships, though, for their depth and continuance. These are your most important as you move through life. Your closest friends offer the chance to feel more connected to the entire world and serve as comrades through the best and worst times. They become inextricably linked to your key memories and help develop your personality and shape your worldview. Choose those friends wisely, curate them well, and do all you can to maintain and nurture your friendships.

The most important relationship you will have, though, is that of your romantic partner. It will be the deepest, hardest, and most meaningful relationship you will have. It isn't easy, but it is worth the work to find and maintain. It compounds fully, changes in nature as you age together. Separation can be the biggest setback you can experience, akin to the death of someone close. With that impact possible, it is imperative that you choose each other wisely and with the purest of intent, allowing yourself to be molded by the other and always acting in each other's best interest. Cliche as it may be, so much truth is found in 1 Corinthians 13.

You are said to be the average of the five closest people to you. Also, it has been proven that one key to individual success is the partner that you choose. Who you surround yourself with will help mold you into the person you will become, for better or worse. You have that same impact on others. Cultivate your tribe and collaborate with them to progress towards long-term success.

Average is your most likely outcome. Plan for it and make it work.

Try as we might to be exceptional, statistically speaking, the majority of us humans, ninety-five percent of us, are going to fall into the average. You can expect and be born with or obtain average intelligence, average ability, average salary, average health, and average life expectancy. If you are above or below average, chances are they will only be in a few areas and only be on the higher or lower end of average, still.

I do not say this to discourage anyone from aiming to be exceptional. I say it to offer encouragement that you are more like all your fellow humans, past and present, and to remind you that great things are accomplished by ordinary people with the conviction, discipline, and focus to pursue great things as normal people. Not every cause is worthy, not every sacrifice is rewarded, but pursuing what you believe in is worth the effort if your expectations of the outcomes, best and worst case, are something you are ok with enduring. Any shot at doing incredible things is a gamble, and every bet is against the house. You may win sometimes, but statistically, the house always wins if you gamble long enough.

The easiest way to cope with this harsh reality and thrive within its seemingly oppressive and nihilistic narrative is to anchor your sense of reality to the average. How would you live if you end up like everyone else by the numbers and maintain your individualism and your personal exceptionalism? The answer is to live a life with a higher purpose and a drive higher than your personal success. It is to anchor your goals to meanings and intentions, rather than material accumulation. They say that if you do what everyone else is doing, you will achieve the same results. When it comes to accumulating money, there is nothing wrong with that. You can look up the average salary, homes, cars, and other markers of success, and how to get them, but not like everyone else does. Not with debt, and stealing from your future success, but with practicality and care.

Keep in mind the larger perspective. If you find yourself in most Western nations, especially the US, the average wealth level here exceeds that of almost all the world substantially. The rest of the world looks to you as the top ten percent. As we expect from the wealthiest in our nation, what are you doing with your wealth and privilege of being born into a place where you can live a comfortable life and add value to those around you?

Work for your future self and be kind to your past self. Do the best you can today.

Imagining our lives in the future is hard. We can expect to live longer than ever before, and things seem to change at a rate faster than ever. Does it really, though? Predictions from fifty to a hundred years ago had all of us in a new utopian state with technological advances that solved energy, labor, and transportation issues, and with those advancements, humans became enlightened, peaceful, and prosperous. Disney's Tomorrowland gave us a visual representation of what the world could be like. However, like the technological advancements they hoped to bring to life, its debut was delayed for budget cuts, released incomplete to the original vision, and eventually was absorbed into the theme park thrills that people asked for over the whimsy of a better future.

We have made humongous technological strides in the last two centuries or so, and they are moving faster every day, thanks to the accuracy of Moore's Law. The social side of things is much slower and much more painful. Society is exhibiting adoption and growing pains in nearly every facet of life. We cannot predict our careers, the economy, or the environment as confidently as we once could. This presents us with great risk and great opportunity, but it requires steadfast diligence to our goals along with flexibility and creativity to adapt. It requires a conscious effort to continue to move forward and not get bogged down in the minutiae of daily life. It requires us to look at ourselves holistically as past, present, and future versions.

Our future self is where all our efforts should be directed. This is the heart and reason of economic thinking. Will what I am doing today help or hurt that future version of me? That really is the only question we need to ask. Asking requires an honest care for that person, though, because it will very likely conflict with what you want today. We do not collect regrets from thinking about doing the best thing in the long run; we have regrets when we prioritize short-term pleasure or risky behaviors against logic, and it works out poorly. We have regrets when we act against our gut that tells us the right thing to do, yet we ignore it.

Our future self is not just the version lying on their deathbed looking back with clarity on our lives; it is us in ten years with more knowledge, wisdom, and responsibility than our current selves. It is our future self that needs or has more resources than you do today because of your movement towards your goals. It is your future self that wishes they could go back in time to tell you not to make that mistake.

They should be kind, though. After all, your future self, as it merges with your current self, is older, wiser, and possesses the gift of hindsight. We all make mistakes. We all make big mistakes from time to time, no matter how hard we try to avoid them. Why we make mistakes is as important as why we do things that produce positive outcomes. Understanding and evaluating our mistakes helps us learn from them and prevents us from making similar mistakes in the future. We have to have the same level of patience, care, and understanding for our past selves as we would with a child we love, allowing them to move on without grudges and animosity against them, giving them room to grow into better people.

Doing the best you can seems passive, but it definitely is not if you take it literally. We often hear "you tried your best" as a consolation when you lose, but did you? Trying your best requires a level of planning, practice, and care. It requires actually giving something all the effort that you possibly can. You should be trying your best at the things that matter. Do not be the best at scrolling on your phone or something that does not enrich your life, but do your best for anything that matters. There is an old saying that "anything worth doing is worth doing right," and it is. Doing things well opens doors to learning and mastery. Skills that you learn from any job that are important enough to land on your to-do list are worth the attention to do it correctly and with care. If your job is to clean a bathroom, imagine the positive impact you can have on someone, like a parent, taking their child to a bathroom, and how helpful it is if it is clean. Imagine the negative effects of a truly disgusting bathroom somewhere you live or work. It seeps out and ruins everyone's experience of being in that building. Your work matters to someone, and it isn't anyone else's job to explain the impact; it is yours, and there is an impact.

Doing your best allows you to test the boundaries of what you are capable of, the level of value you can add, and it signals to the world what you are capable of. It is one of the highest morals you can hold, not for some puritan pitch of work ethic, but for signaling to yourself that you are competent, because no one needs to see and believe that more than you. Don't let your future version down by not applying yourself and building the skills needed to show up, try hard, and succeed.

In conclusion, our lives, our finances, and our overall happiness can be as complicated as we choose to make them. There is no shortage of things to integrate or choose, with good reason, that add layers of complexity to our lives in efforts to improve various aspects and produce desired outcomes. From technological integration that helps you be more productive and get more done, more education to secure a more technical career, making high-risk investments in efforts to secure more capital, or even planning your relationships and family to match your desired life structure. There is no right or wrong choice for these things at face value. After all, your definition of success and strategy to achieve it in life is as unique as your personal finance plan. No one else can plan it for you, nor execute towards it.

What it all boils down to is your conviction and your intent. Your conviction of what is right. I believe we are all born with the programming available intrinsically and through osmosis with our society to discern right from wrong. We are surrounded by rules and laws that guide us towards things as simple as do not steal, do not kill, and the golden rule. Even with that, there is as much incentive to abandon these core principles in ways that serve us in the short-term. Contentment breeds happiness, and contentment comes from your ability to assess your actions and outcomes and find them in balance with your utmost effort and directed by your own moral compass. Are you doing your best, and are you doing what is right? A lot of things will sort themselves out by being able to answer yes to those two questions.

Better decisions are made by accumulating knowledge. It is hard to make forward-looking decisions with no research or education on the matter, so honing your understanding constantly to ensure you are making the most informed decisions possible and looking forward to assessing how they will benefit or could hurt your future self. You will make mistakes, and the best you can do is try to mitigate their impact, fix things, and learn from them to avoid similar ones in the future. Those experiences are what culminate as your wisdom, and it is one of the most valuable assets you can accumulate in your life's portfolio: broad, applicable, and acknowledged wisdom.

None of this is achieved quickly, so you must be patient. I wish luck to everyone and hope that fortune favors people financially and in life's endeavors, but I discourage any of us from planning on these things. Instead, I hope that we have realistic goals that leave room to responsibly manage windfalls of luck and success, apply them to our goals, and not be swayed by increasing needs and wants. Our success should help achieve our goals and enable us to be charitable with our excess to assist others, paying that fortune forward.

We are all in this together. Humans were not meant to be alone, and we are not made to serve only ourselves. We thrive when we struggle together and share success. We grow when we give back and deepen our relationships through actions and care. Gratitude is so much sweeter when we can attribute much of the good in our lives to those we share it with, acknowledging that we are a valuable part of a much bigger picture.

So plan your route, pursue happiness, be content, and grow your own sphere of influence. Do this to optimize your gifts and success, and not to maximize your appearance of success. There is a certain amount of self-interest that we have to hold to do this, because you cannot help anyone if you cannot first help yourself. Your success requires you to have a tribe that supports your growth until you are self-sufficient and can give back, starting the cycle for others.

As you grow, you take on more relationships, more responsibility, and you begin to build your wealth within your network. Grow your connections as wide and deep as you can manage. Size is not the important thing; it is the impact. Much as your talents develop uniquely to you, so does the way you impact the world. Some are adept at adding a little value to a large number of people. Some are talented in adding large amounts of value to a few. Both sides have a time, place, and application, and there are times that you will need to work at both the breadth and depth of your relationships, because one thing is certain, and that is without some level of both, you will suffer.

So do not be afraid or disappointed in who you are, average as you may be. I assure you, most of us are average in most regards, ninety percent of us or so in a big world. We are the masses, and others are outliers. Even if it doesn't feel like it at times, the world is made for us. Without those who work and buy, businesses would not exist. All products are built for the largest market, all governments fear their citizens the most, and individualism is possibly the biggest marketing ploy of all.

You are very special and unique, and what makes you that way is your approach to the average. Your unique set of attributes, working in concert with other average individuals.

I hope that you always feel in control of your own destiny, because, possibly more than ever in history, you are. You are free to learn anything and apply yourself in almost any way. You can build your opinions, skills, and style in your own unique ways and build a life of relative comfort. You can choose, now more than ever, to live like no one else and not conform. If you live like everyone else, you can expect the same results, and, quite frankly, things are not working out well for most because of this. Our jealousy and lack of creativity stunts our growth and success. Our wants for more are based on what we know is available and not what we need.

Temperance is the best safeguard for our happiness. Be patient and try not to want too much of what you do not need. The great thing about originality and freedom is that we get to define what success is to us without outside input, and we can be creative in how we get there.

I hope that when you take out your index card, it is different from mine or anyone else's. Most of all, I hope that you are inspired to embrace being average and can relieve some of the weight that we all feel to be exceptional in the eyes of the world, and know that true wealth can be accumulated at any level of income. I hope that you would be encouraged to not feel pressure to acquire more signals of wealth, but unique ways to build it into your character.

We have enough stuff, but seem to be losing a bit of the character that led to the success of today's world, making it harder to harness the advances we are privileged to implement into our lives. In these times of increasing complexity and comfort, keeping things simple and nurturing our humanity is about the only thing we can do to maintain our sanity and effectiveness long-term. So, embrace the world as it is, be kind to yourself and others, and in the words of the beloved Dr. Spock, "live long and prosper."

REFERENCES

[1] *Private Pension Plans*. Social Security Administration. https://www.ssa.gov/policy/docs/ssb/v39n6/v39n6p3.pdf

[2] "Measures of Central Tendency for Wage Data." *Social Security Administration*, www.ssa.gov/oact/cola/central.html.

[3] "September 2024 Update to the Poverty and Inequality Platform (PIP)." *World Bank Group*, Sept. 2024, https://documents1.worldbank.org/curated/en/099913509172439457/pdf/IDU1332880781f0f4147051b5f81765fe1a1bd77.pdf#:~:text=The%20September%202024%20update%20to%20the%20Poverty%20and,these%20changes%20and%20the%20methodological%20reasons%20behind%20them

[4] "National Study of Millionaires 2024 - The American Dream Is Still Alive." *Ramsey Solutions* https://documents1.worldbank.org/curated/en/099913509172439457/pdf/IDU1332880781f0f4147051b5f81765fe1a1bd77.pdf#:~:text=The%20September%202024%20update%20to%20the%20Poverty%20and,these%20changes%20and%20the%20methodological%20reasons%20behind%20them

[5] "Prevalence, Correlates, Disability, and Comorbidity of DSM-IV Narcissistic Personality Disorder: Results from the Wave 2 National Epidemiologic Survey on Alcohol and Related Conditions." *National Library of Medicine*, 1 Jul. 2009, https://pmc.ncbi.nlm.nih.gov/articles/PMC2669224/

[6] "The Natural History of Antisocial Personality Disorder." *National Library of Medicine*, 7 Jul. 2015, pmc.ncbi.nlm.nih.gov/articles/PMC2669224/.

[7] "Planning & Progress Study 2022." *Northwest Mutual*, Jan. 2023, https://news.northwesternmutual.com/planning-and-progress-study-2022

[8] "2023 Report." *Economic Well-Being of U.S. Households in 2023*, May 2024, www.federalreserve.gov/publications/files/2023-report-economic-well-being-us-households-202405.pdf.
Via: "The Average Savings Account Balance." *The Motley Fool*, 12 May 2025, www.fool.com/money/research/average-savings-account-balance/.

[9] "NCHS Data Brief No. 521, December 2024." *National Center for Health Statistics*, Dec. 2024, www.cdc.gov/nchs/products/databriefs/db521.htm.

[10] "Average IQ by Country 2025." *World Population Review*, 2024, https://worldpopulationreview.com/country-rankings/average-iq-by-country Accessed Jul. 2025.

[11] Kruger, J., & Dunning, D. (1999). Unskilled and unaware of it: how difficulties in recognizing ones own incompetence lead to inflated self-assessments. Journal of Personality and Social Psychology, 77(6), 1121.

[12] Sethi, Ramit. I Will Teach You to Be Rich: No Guilt. No Excuses. No BS. Just a 6-Week Program That Works. 2nd ed., Workman Publishing Company, 2019.

[13] "Forbes 2025 Billionaires List." *Forbes*, 2025, www.forbes.com/billionaires/. Accessed Jul. 2025.

[14] Kahneman, Daniel, and Angus Deaton. "High Income Improves Evaluation of Life but Not Emotional Well-being." *The Proceedings of the National Academy of Sciences (PNAS)*, 7 Sept. 2010, www.pnas.org/doi/full/10.1073/pnas.1011492107.

[15] "Bureau of Labor Statistics April 23, 2025 News Release." *Bureau of Labor Statistics*, 23 Apr. 2025, www.bls.gov/news.release/pdf/famee.pdf.

[16] Fry, Richard, et al. "In a Growing Share of U.S. Marriages, Husbands and Wives Earn About the Same." *Pew Research*, 13 Apr. 2023, www.pewresearch.org/social-trends/2023/04/13/in-a-growing-share-of-u-s-marriages-husbands-and-wives-earn-about-the-same/.

[17] Kaplan, Robert M., and Richard G. Kronik. "Marital Status and Longevity in the United States Population." *National Library of Medicine, PubMed Central*, Sept. 2006, https://pmc.ncbi.nlm.nih.gov/articles/PMC2566023/

[18] "Sbarra, David A., and Paul J. Nietert. "Divorce and Death: Forty Years of the Charleston Heart Study." *National Library of Medicine, PubMed Central*, Dec. 2008, https://pmc.ncbi.nlm.nih.gov/articles/PMC2977944/

[19] "The Joy of Intimacy: A Soulful Guide to Love, Sexuality, and Marriage" by Manis Friedman and Ricardo Adler

[20] Allendorf, Keera. "Determinants of Marital Quality in an Arranged Marriage Society." *National Library of Medicine, PubMed Central*, Jul. 2015, https://pmc.ncbi.nlm.nih.gov/articles/PMC3711098/

[21] Schwartz, Barry, 1946-. The Paradox of Choice : Why More Is Less. New York :Ecco, 2004.

[22] Palahniuk, Chuck. Fight Club. Vintage Books, 2007.

[23] "Forbes Profile: Warren Buffett." *Forbes*, www.forbes.com/profile/warren-buffett/. Accessed Aug. 2025.

[24] "Contraceptive Deserts: Lack of Access = Lack of Power to Decide." *Power to Decide*, 1 Jul. 2015, powertodecide.org/what-we-do/contraceptive-deserts. Accessed May 2025.

[25] "About Teen Pregnancy." *Center for Desease Control*, 15 May 2024, www.cdc.gov/reproductive-health/teen-pregnancy/index.html.

[26] National Academies of Sciences, Engineering, and Medicine;Health and Medicine Division;Board on Population Health and Public Health Practice;Committee on Prevention and Control of Sexually Transmitted Infections in the United States; Crowley JS, Geller AB, Vermund SH, editors. Sexually Transmitted Infections: Adopting a Sexual Health Paradigm. Washington (DC): National Academies Press (US); 2021 Mar 24. Available from: https://www.ncbi.nlm.nih.gov/books/NBK573154/ doi: 10.17226/25955

[27] Wolfinger, Nicholas H. "Counterintuitive Trends in the Link Between Premarital Sex and Marital Stability." *Institute for Family Studies*, 2 Sept. 2016, https://ifstudies.org/ifs-admin/resources/counterintuitive-trends-in-the-link-between-premarital-sex-and-marital-stability-family-studiesfamily-studies.pdf

[28] "Women More Likely Than Men to Initiate Divorces, But Not Non-Marital Breakups." *American Sociological Association*, 22 Aug. 2015, www.asanet.org/women-more-likely-men-initiate-divorces-not-non-marital-breakups/.

[29] Vandenbroucke, Guillaume. "The Effect of Divorce on Workers' Incomes." *Federal Reserve Bank of St. Louis*, 5 Feb. 2024, www.stlouisfed.org/on-the-economy/2024/feb/effect-divorce-workers-incomes#:~:text=On%20average%2C%20the%20difference%20is,worth%20pondering%20in%20future%20research.https://www2.census.gov/library/working-papers/2025/adrm/ces/CES-WP-25-28.pdf.

[30] Livingston, Gretchen. "Four-in-Ten Couples Are Saying "I Do," Again Chapter 2: The Demographics of Remarriage." *Pew Research Center*, 14 Nov. 2014, www.pewresearch.org/social-trends/2014/11/14/chapter-2-the-demographics-of-remarriage/#:~:text=The%20increasing%20prevalence%20of%20remarriage,%25%20of%20foreign%2Dborn%20adults.

[31] Leithead, Katie. "FALSE REPORTS – PERCENTAGE." *End Violence Against Women International*, 5 Oct. 2021, https://evawintl.org/best_practice_faqs/false-reports-percentage/#:~:text=However%2C%20estimates%20narrow%20to%20the,and%20validity%20of%20the%20research

And

Roman, John, et al. "Post-Conviction DNA Testing and Wrongful Conviction." *Urban Institute*, 18 Jun. 2012, www.urban.org/research/publication/post-conviction-dna-testing-and-wrongful-conviction.

[32] "The Eighth United Nations Survey on Crime Trends and the Operations of Criminal Justice Systems (2001 - 2002)." *United Nations*, Aug. 2023, www.unodc.org/unodc/en/data-and-analysis/Eighth-United-Nations-Survey-on-Crime-Trends-and-the-Operations-of-Criminal-Justice-Systems.html.

[33] "Statistics About Sexual Violence." *National Sexual Violence Resource Center*, www.nsvrc.org/sites/default/files/publications_nsvrc_factsheet_media-packet_statistics-about-sexual-violence_0.pdf. Accessed May 2025.

[34] Fanelli, Daniele. "How Many Scientists Fabricate and Falsify Research? A Systematic Review and Meta-Analysis of Survey Data." *The University of Edinburgh*, May 2009, www.research.ed.ac.uk/en/publications/how-many-scientists-fabricate-and-falsify-research-a-systematic-r
Via:
https://www.pure.ed.ac.uk/ws/portalfiles/portal/8079953/2009_How_Many_Scientists_Fabricate_and_Falsify_Research.pdf.

[35] Liu, Junxiu MD, et al. "Association of Coffee Consumption With All-Cause and Cardiovascular Disease Mortality." *Mayo Clinic Proceedings*, Oct. 2013, www.mayoclinicproceedings.org/article/S0025-6196%2813%2900578-8/fulltext.

[36] Olen, H., & Pollack, H. (2016). The index card: Why personal finance doesn't have to be complicated. Portfolio/Penguin.

ABOUT THE AUTHOR

By the numbers alone, Reid was below average in most aspects. growing up and would seem to have low potential for any kind of success. With little formal education from a young age and growing up in a low-income home, he had very few examples to reference when it came to the building blocks of success and material security. Regardless, he pressed forward and managed to obtain an education, a respectable career, and build a stable and thriving family, figuring each step out along the way.

In his career, he has focused on one thing: helping normal people achieve more. Whether transitioning family businesses from paper records to software, translating complicated requirements into easy-to-adopt systems, or helping tech companies maximize engagement with the widest possible set of users, he knows that there are human elements that cannot be ignored if you hope to thrive with the average population.

Now, he hopes to share his experiences with those like him, the average young person just trying to figure things out. Career, finance, faith, and relationships are the building blocks for true success, and each is getting more complicated by the day. He is constantly breaking down the basics, hoping to help others implement good frameworks into their lives, with the result being able to define and achieve success on their own terms.

As a father and a big brother, he brings empathetic, but harshly realistic topics to his audience with the sole intention of helping others make their corner of the world just a little bit better.

Discover more books and content from the author at
lifeofcompoundinginterest.com